List of Statutory Instruments

together with the List of Statutory Rules
of Northern Ireland
for the month of

April 1998

Contents

Preface iii
List of abbreviations iv
Out of print publications v
Standing order service v
Customer service vi
List of statutory instruments by subject headings 179
Numerical list of statutory instruments with subject headings 197
List of statutory instruments having subsidiary numbers 200
Alphabetical index of statutory instruments 201
List of statutory rules of Northern Ireland 241
List of statutory rules of Northern Ireland by subject headings 243
Numerical list of statutory rules of Northern Ireland with subject headings . . . 247
List of statutory rules of Northern Ireland having commencement order nos. . . . 247
Alphabetical index of statutory rules of Northern Ireland 248
Stationery Office information and services vii
Enquiries viii
Orders ix
SI-CD ROM & British Standards information x
The Stationery Office Ltd terms & conditions of sale xi

ISBN 011 500580 3
ISSN 0267-2979

London: The Stationery Office

© Crown Copyright 1998
Applications for reproduction should be made to The Copyright Unit, Her Majesty's Stationery Office, St Clement's House, 2-16 Colegate, Norwich NR3 1BQ

Printed in the UK for The Stationery Office Limited under the authority and superintendence of Carol Tullo, Controller of Her Majesty's Stationery Office and Queen's Printer of Acts of Parliament

Preface

This *List* contains:

(a) a list of the general and local statutory instruments (printed and non-printed) issued in the month, arranged under subject headings. Each entry includes, where available or appropriate: the enabling power, as set out in italics; the date when the instrument was issued, made and laid and comes into force; a short note of any effect; territorial extent and classification; pagination; ISBN and price;

(b) a numerical list of the same instruments, with their subject headings;

(c) a list of instruments which have subsidiary numbers (C for commencement orders; L for instruments relating to court fees or procedure in England and Wales; NI for orders in Council relating only to Northern Ireland; S for instruments that extend only to Scotland);

(d) an alphabetical subject index;

(e) a list of Northern Ireland statutory rules and associated indexes.

Details of later statutory instruments may be found in the monthly *List of Statutory Instruments*. The *Daily List* of publications from the Stationery Office contains particulars only of those issued by the Stationery Office. Details of previous years' annual lists which are still available appear on the inside back cover.

The full text of the general statutory instruments appears in the annual edition of *Statutory Instruments*. This is issued in three consecutive parts, each of which has an index and table of effects. Part III also contains a classified list of the local statutory instruments (both printed and non-printed).

Copies of local instruments issued recently by The Stationery Office Limited may be obtained from the addresses on the back cover. Copies of local instruments unobtainable from The Stationery Office may be obtained at prevailing prices from

- Her Majesty's Stationery Office, Statutory Publications Section, 67 Tufton Street, London SW1P 3QS (from 1922 onwards – except for the years 1942, 1950, 1951 and up to SI no. 940 of 1952)
- Head of Search Department, Public Record Office, Chancery Lane, London WC2A 1LR (as before, up to 1960)
- British Library, Official Publications and Social Sciences Service, Great Russell Street, London WC1B 3DG (as before, up to 1980)

To find out what general statutory instruments are in force on a given subject, or under a particular act, refer to the *Index to Government Orders*. This is published every two years, with a supplement in the intervening year. To ascertain whether a particular general statutory instrument is still in force, refer to the *Table of Government Orders* published annually with a noter-up during its currency. Alternatively, contact The Stationery Office enquiries section (see p. viii).

The publications referred to in this catalogue shall be supplied to the customer only on the Stationery Office Ltd.'s terms and conditions of sale (see p. xi-xii) and not on any additional terms which may be included with the customer's order.

Prices are subject to change without notice.

List of abbreviations

accord.	accordance
art(s).	article(s)
c.	chapter
C.	Commencement
C.I.	Channel Islands
E.	England
EEC	European Economic Community
G.	Guernsey
G.B.	Great Britain
GLC	Greater London Council
IOM	Isle of Man
J.	Jersey
L.	Legal: fees or procedure in courts in E. & W.
N.I.	Northern Ireland*
para(s).	paragraph(s)
reg(s).	regulation(s)
s(s).	section(s)
S.	Scotland
sch(s).	schedule(s)
S.I.	Statutory instrument(s)
S.R.	Statutory rule(s) of Northern Ireland
S.R. & O.	Statutory rules and orders
U.K.	United Kingdom
W.	Wales

* Northern Ireland: to distinguish between acts of Parliament (Westminster) and acts of the Northern Ireland Parliament (Stormont) the former are shown Year Chapter no. (N.I), and the latter Year (N.I.) Chapter no.

Out-of-print publications

Photocopies of out-of-print Parliamentary, statutory and regulatory publications can be obtained by the Stationery Office from the British Library Document Supply Centre. Customers requiring this service should order through

  The Stationery Office Ltd (Photocopies section)
  PO Box 276
  London SW8 5DT
  (Tel. 0171 873 8455)

The section will advise the current rate for this service.

Copyright

Most Stationery Office publications are Crown or Parliamentary copyright. Letters of guidance for publishers and librarians on the circumstances where it is necessary to request permission to reproduce Crown or Parliamentary copyright material are available from the following address (to which requests for permission to reproduce material should also be sent). The letters can also be found on the Internet at *http://www.hmso.gov.uk*.

  Her Majesty's Stationery Office
  Copyright Unit
  St Clements House
  2-16 Colegate
  Norwich NR3 1BQ
  (Tel. 01603 621000; Fax 01603 723000)

The Stationery Office's Standing Order Service

The Standing Order Service, open to all account holders, allows you to receive automatically the publications you require in a specified subject area. This saves you the time, trouble and expense of placing individual orders.

The subject classifications used are specific enough to allow very precise targeting of subject areas, and are revised from time to time to meet changing needs.

For more information please contact our Standing Orders department on 0870 600 5522, or fax us on 0870 600 5533.

Customer Service

We aim to provide a courteous and efficient service at all times. We have set targets for our service to our customers and monitor the performance achieved.

MAIL, TELEPHONE AND FAX ORDERS

We aim to despatch publications to customers within five days of receiving an order. Goods are despatched in accordance with our terms & conditions of sale.

STANDING ORDERS

We aim to despatch all standing order publications within two days of publication date.

SUBSCRIPTIONS

We aim to despatch all subscription publications on or before the day of publication.

PROBLEMS

If you have not received your goods and would like to ask about your order, or if you have already received your order and found it unsatisfactory in any way, please contact The Stationery Office address to which your order was sent. The addresses and telephone numbers are given on the back cover of this catalogue.

QUALITY

The Stationery Office's quality policy is to earn a reputation for excellence in satisfying customers' expectations through continual improvement and innovations.

We welcome comments on our service, and any suggestions for improvement

LIST OF STATUTORY INSTRUMENTS BY SUBJECT HEADING

AGRICULTURE

The Agriculture Act 1986 (Commencement no. 6) Order 1998 No. 879 (C. 19). Enabling power: *Agriculture Act 1986, c. 24 (2). Bringing into operation various provisions of the 1986 Act on 01.04.1998* Issued: 06.04.1998. Made: 19.03.1998. Effect: None. Territorial extent & classification: E/W/S/NI. General. – 2p. – 0 11 065870 1 *£0.65*

The Fertilisers (Mammalian Meat and Bone Meal) (Conditions of Manufacture) Regulations 1998 No. 955. Enabling power: *European Communities Act 1972, s. 2 (2)* Issued: 16.04.1998. Made: 02.04.1998. Laid: 03.04.1998. Coming into force: 30.04.1998. Effect: None. Territorial extent & classification:E/W/S. General. – 6p. – 0 11 065911 2 *£1.55*

The Fertilisers (Mammalian Meat and Bone Meal) Regulations 1998 No. 954. Enabling power: *Agriculture Act 1970, s. 74A (1), 84 (1)* Issued: 16.04.1998. Made: 02.04.1998. Laid: 03.04.1998. Coming into force: 30.04.1998. Effect: S.I. 1996/1125, 2473 revoked. Territorial extent & classification: E/W/S. General. – 4p. – 0 11 065912 0 *£1.10*

ANIMALS: ANIMAL HEALTH

The Cattle Identification Regulations 1998 No. 871. Enabling power: *European Communities Act 1972, s. 2 (2)* Issued: 22.04.1998. Made: 19.03.1998. Laid: 20.03.1998. Coming into force: 15.04.1998. Effect: S.I. 1993/1441; 1995/12; 1996/3241 amended & S.I. 1996/1686, 2255; 1997/1901 revoked (1996/1686 revoked with savings). Territorial extent & classification: E/W/S. General. – Implements for Great Britain provisions of REG (EC) 820/97; (EC) 2628/97; (EC) 2929/97 - regarding labelling of beef & beef products, eartags, holding registers & passports. –20p. – 0 11 065931 7 *£3.70*

ANTARCTICA

The Antarctic (Amendment) Regulations 1998 No. 1007. Enabling power: *Antarctic Act 1994, s. 9(1), 10(1), 11(1), 14(1), 15(c), 25(1)(3), 32* Issued: 28.04.1998. Made: 19.04.1998. Laid: 08.04.1998. Coming into force: 01.05.1998. Effect: S.I. 1995/490 amended. Territorial extent & classification: E/W/S/NI. General. – 20p. – 0 11 065942 2 *£3.70*

BETTING, GAMING AND LOTTERIES

The Gaming Act (Variation of Monetary Limits) Order 1998 No. 962. Enabling power: *Gaming Act 1968, ss. 20 (3) (8), 51 (4)* Issued: 17.04.1998. Made: 02.04.1998. Laid: 17.04.1998. Coming into force: 11.05.1998. Effect: S.I. 1995/926, 1020 amended. Territorial extent & classification: E/W/S. General. – 2p. – 0 11 065894 9 *£0.65*

The Gaming Clubs (Hours and Charges) (Amendment) Regulations 1998 No. 961. Enabling power: *Gaming Act 1968, ss. 14 (2), 51* Issued: 17.04.1998. Made: 02.04.1998. Laid: 17.04.1998. Coming into force: 11.05.1998. Effect: S.I. 1984/248, 470 amended & 1996/1109, 1144 revoked. Territorial extent & classification: E/W/S. General. – 2p. – 0 11 065895 7 *£0.65*

BUILDING SOCIETIES

The Building Societies (General Charge and Fees) Regulations 1998 No. 675. Enabling power: *Building Societies Act 1986, ss. 2(2)(4), 116(2)* Issued: 06.04.1998. Made: 11.03.1998. Laid: 11.03.1998. Coming into force: 01.04.1998. Effect: S.I. 1997/740 revoked. Territorial extent & classification: E/W/S/NI. General. – 8p. – 0 11 065868 X *£1.95*

CABS

The London Cab Order 1998 No. 1043. Enabling power: *Metropolitan Public Carriage Act 1869, s. 9, London Cab and Stage Carriage Act 1907, s.1, & London Cab Act 1968, s. 1* Issued: 23.04.1998. Made: 04.04.1998. Coming into force: 25.04.1998. Effect: S.R. & O. 1934/1346 amended. Territorial extent & classification: E. Local. 2p. 0 11 065927 9 *£0.65*

CHANNEL TUNNEL

The Channel Tunnel (Carriers' Liability) Order 1998 No. 1015. Enabling power: *Channel Tunnel Act 1987, s. 11* Issued: 22.04.1998. Made: 08.04.1998. Laid: 08.04.1998. Coming into force: 09.04.1998. Effect: 1978 c. 24 amended. Territorial extent & classification: UK. General. – 4p. – 0 11 065929 5 *£1.10*

CIVIL AVIATION

The Air Navigation (Restriction of Flying) (Chippenham) Regulations 1998 No. 327. Enabling power: *S.I. 1995/1970, art. 75.* Made: 13.02.1998. Coming into force: 13.02.1998. Effect: None. Revoked by 1998/328 unpublished. – *Unpublished*

The Air Navigation (Restriction of Flying) (Chippenham) (Revocation) Regulations 1998 No.328. Enabling power: *S.I. 1995/1970, art. 75.* Made: 15.02.1998. Coming into force: 15.02.1998. Effect: S.I. 1998/327 revoked. – *Unpublished*

The Air Navigation (Restriction of Flying) (Dover) Regulations 1998 No. 318. Enabling power: *S.I. 1995/1970, art. 75.* Made: 10.02.1998. Coming into force: 28.02.1998. Effect: None. – *Unpublished*

Prices/availability are liable to change without notice

180 *CUSTOMS AND EXCISE*

The Air Navigation (Restriction of Flying) (Exhibition of Flying) Regulations 1998 No.316. Enabling power: *S.I. 1995/1970, art. 75.* Made: 09.02.1998. Coming into force: 06.03.1998. Effect: None. – *Unpublished*

The Air Navigation (Restriction of Flying) (Perth) Regulations 1998 No. 317. Enabling power: *S.I. 1995/1970, art. 75.* Made: 09.02.1998. Coming into force: 05.03.1998. Effect: None. – *Unpublished*

The Air Navigation (Restriction of Flying) (Portadown) Regulations 1998 No. 315. Enabling power: *S.I. 1995/1970, art. 75.* Made: 06.02.1998. Coming into force: 17.03.1998. Effect: None. – *Unpublished*

The Carriage by Air Acts (Application of Provisions) (Fourth Amendment) Order 1998 No.1058. Enabling power: *Carriage by Air Act 1961, s. 10.* Issued: 30.04.1998. Made: 22.04.1998. Coming into force: 02.05.1998. In accord. with art. 1. Effect: S.I. 1967/480 amended. Territorial extent & classification: E/W/S/NI. General. – Supersedes draft SI ISBN 0110654161 issued on 29.01.1998. – 16p. – 0 11 065949 X *£3.20*

The Civil Aviation Act 1982 (Jersey) (Amendment) Order 1998 No. 748. Enabling power: *Civil Aviation Act 1982, s. 108 (1)* Issued: 02.04.1998. Made: 18.03.1998. Coming into force: 18.05.1998. Effect: S.I. 1990/2145 amended. Territorial extent & classification: Jersey. General. This SI has been made in consequence of defects in S.I. 1990/2145 and is being issued free of charge to all known recipients of that Statutory Instrument. The original SI under ISBN 0110051459 is available via our On Demand Service. – 2p. – 0 11 065862 0 *£0.65*

CONSTRUCTION CONTRACTS

The Construction Contracts (Scotland) Exclusion Order 1998 No. 686 (S. 33). Enabling power: *Housing Grants, Construction and Regeneration Act 1996, ss. 106 (1) (b), 146 (1)* Issued: 02.04.1998. Made: 06.03.1998. Coming into force: 01.05.1998. Effect: None. Territorial extent & classification: S. General. – 4p. – 0 11 055747 6 *£1.10*

The Housing Grants, Construction and Regeneration Act 1996 (Scotland) (Commencement No. 5) Order 1998 No. 894 (C. 20) (S. 47). Enabling power: *Housing Grants, Construction and Regeneration Act 1996, s. 150 (3). Bringing into operation various provisions of the 1996 Act on 01.05.1998* Issued: 17.04.1998. Made: 19.03.1998. Effect: None. Territorial extent & classification: S. General. – 4p. – 0 11 055755 7 *£1.10*

The Scheme for Construction Contracts (Scotland) Regulations 1998 No. 687 (S. 34). Enabling power: *Housing Grants, Construction and Regeneration Act 1996, ss. 108 (6), 114, 146* Issued: 02.04.1998. Made: 06.03.1998. Coming into force: 01.05.1998. Effect: None. Territorial extent & classification: S. General. – 8p. – 0 11 055746 8 *£1.95*

CONSUMER CREDIT

The Consumer Credit (Further Increase of Monetary Amounts) Order 1998 No. 997. Enabling power: *Consumer Credit Act 1974, s. 181 (1)* Issued: 20.04.1998. Made: 31.03.1998. Laid: 08.04.1998. Coming into force: 01.05.1998. Effect: S.I. 1983/1571 revoked. Territorial extent & classification: E/W/S/NI. General. – 4p. – 0 11 065924 4 *£1.10*

The Consumer Credit (Increase of Monetary Limits) (Amendment) Order 1998 No. 996. Enabling power: *Consumer Credit Act 1974, s. 181 (1)* Issued: 20.04.1998. Made: 31.03.1998. Coming into force: 01.05.1998. Effect: S.I. 1983/1878 amended. Territorial extent & classification: E/W/S/NI. General. – 2p. – 0 11 065923 6 *£0.65*

The Consumer Credit (Realisation of Pawn) (Amendment) Regulations 1998 No. 998. Enabling power: *Consumer Credit Act 1974, ss. 121 (1), 189 (1)* Issued: 20.04.1998. Made: 01.04.1998. Laid: 08.04.1998. Coming into force: 01.05.1998. Effect: S.I. 1983/1568 revoked. Territorial extent & classification: E/W/S/NI. General. – 2p. – 0 11 065925 2 *£0.65*

COURT OF SESSION, SCOTLAND

Act of Sederunt (Rules of the Court of Session Amendment) (Miscellaneous) 1998 No.890 (S. 45). Enabling power: *Court of Session Act 1998, s. 5* Issued: 09.04.1998. Made: 19.03.1998. Coming into force: 21.04.1998. Effect: S.I. 1994/1443 amended. Territorial extent & classification: S. General. – 8p. – 0 11 055757 3 *£1.95*

Act of Sederunt (Rules of the Court of Session Amendment No. 2) (Fees of Shorthand Writers) 1998 No. 993 (S. 56). Enabling power: *Court of Session Act 1988, s. 5* Issued: 22.04.1998. Made: 01.04.1998. Coming into force: 01.05.1998. Effect: S.I. 1994/1443 amended. Territorial extent & classification: S. General. – 4p. – 0 11 055768 9 *£1.10*

CRIMINAL LAW, SCOTLAND

The Proceeds of Crime (Scotland) Act 1995 (Enforcement of Northern Ireland Orders) Order 1998 No. 752 (S. 42). Enabling power: *Proceeds of Crime (Scotland) Act 1995, s. 39* Issued: 16.04.1998. Made: 18.03.1998. Laid: 30.03.1998. Coming into force: 01.05.1998. Effect: None. Territorial extent & classification: S. General. – 4p. – 0 11 055754 9 *£1.10*

CUSTOMS AND EXCISE

The Dual-use and Related Goods (Export Control) (Amendment No. 2) Regulations 1998 No.899. Enabling power: *European Communities Act 1972, s. 2 (2)* Issued: 09.04.1998. Made: 26.03.1998. Laid: 30.03.1998. Coming into force: 24.04.1998. Effect: S.I. 1996/2721 amended. Territorial extent & classification: E/W/S/NI. General. – 2p. – 0 11 065886 8 *£0.65*

EDUCATION, ENGLAND AND WALES

The Education (Grant-maintained and Grant-maintained Special Schools) (Finance) Regulations 1998 No. 799. Enabling power: *Education Act 1996. ss. 244 (2), 245, 246 (1) (2), . 247 (2), 257, 569 (4) (5)* Issued: 06.04.1998. Made: 26.03.1998. Laid: 27.03.1998. Coming into force: 01.04.1998. Effect: S.I. 1997/996 revoked. Territorial extent & classification: E/W. General. – 30p. – 0 11 065881 7 *£5.60*

The Education (Individual Pupils' Achievements) (Information) (Amendment) Regulations 1998 No. 877. Enabling power: *Education Act 1996, ss. 408, 569 (4) (5)* Issued: 07.04.1998. Made: 18.03.1998. Laid: 24.03.1998. Coming into force: 14.04.1998. Effect: S.I. 1997/1368 amended. Territorial extent & classification: E/W. General. – 4p. – 0 11 065884 1 *£1.10*

The Education (New Grant-maintained Schools) (Finance) Regulations 1998 No. 798. Enabling power: *Education Act 1996, ss. 244 (2), 245, 246 (1) (2), 247 (2) (6), 257, 569 (4) (5)* Issued: 01.04.1998. Made: 25.03.1998. Laid: 25.03.1998. Coming into force: 01.04.1998. Effect: S.I. 1997/956 revoked. Territorial extent & classification: E/W. General. – 20p. – 0 11 065861 2 *£3.70*

The Education (Publication of Local Education Authority Insppection Reports) Regulations 1998 No. 880. Enabling power: *Education Act 1997, s. 39 (3)* Issued: 03.04.1998. Made: 23.03.1998. Laid: 24.03.1998. Coming into force: 14.04.1998. Effect: None. Territorial extent & classification: E/W. General. – 4p. – 0 11 065872 8 *£1.10*

The Education (School Teachers' Pay and Conditions) Order 1998 No. 903. Enabling power: *School Teachers' Pay and Conditions Act 1991, ss. 2 (1) (3) (4), 5 (4)* Issued: 03.04.1998. Made: 30.03.1998. Laid: 30.03.1998. Coming into force: 20.04.1998. Effect: None. Territorial extent & classification: E/W. General. – 8p. – 0 11 065871 X *£1.95*

The Nursery Education (England) Regulations 1998 No. 655. Correction slip, dated April 1998. – *Free*

EDUCATION, SCOTLAND

The Teachers (Compensation for Premature Retirement and Redundancy) (Scotland) Amendment Regulations 1998 No. 719 (S. 37). Enabling power: *Superannuation Act 1972, s.24* Issued: 02.04.1998. Made: 04.03.1998. Laid: 24.03.1998. Coming into force: 15.04.1998. Effect: S.I. 1996/2317 amended. Territorial extent & classification: S. General. – 2p. – 0 11 055749 2 *£0.65*

The Teachers' Superannuation (Scotland) Amendment Regulations 1998 No. 718 (S. 36). Enabling power: *Superannuation Act 1972, sch.3, ss. 9, 12* Issued: 02.04.1998. Made: 04.03.1998. Laid: 24.03.1998. Coming into force: 15.04.1998. Effect: 1992/280 amended. Territorial extent & classification: S. General. – With correction slip, dated April 1998. – 24p. – 0 11 055748 4 *£4.15*

ELECTRICITY

The Fossil Fuel Levy Act 1998 (Commencement) Order 1998 No. 930 (C. 21). Enabling power: *Fossil Fuel Levy Act 1998, s. 2 (2). Bringing into operation the Act on 01/04/1998.* Issued: 20.04.1998. Made: 31.03.1998. Effect: None. Territorial extent & classification: E/W/S. General. – 2p. – 0 11 065922 8 *£0.65*

ENVIRONMENTAL PROTECTION

The Environment Act 1995 (Commencement no. 12 and Transitional Provisions) (Scotland) Order 1998 No. 781 (S. 40) (C. 16). Enabling power: *Environment Act 1995, s. 125 (3) (4). Bringing into operation various provisions of the 1995 act on 08.04.1998* Issued: 08.04.1998. Made: 11.30.1998. Effect: None. Territorial extent & classification: S. General. – 6p. – 0 11 055753 0 *£1.55*

The Financial Assistance for Environmental Purposes (No. 3) Order 1998 No. 1001. Enabling power: *Environmental Protection Act 1990, s. 153 (4)* Issued: 21.04.1998. Made: 07.04.1998. Laid: 08.04.1998. Coming into force: 24.04.1998. except art. 3 which comes into force on 23.04.1998. Effect: 1990 c. 43 amended & S.I. 1998/946 revoked prior to publication. Territorial extent & classification: E/W/S. General. – 2p. – 0 11 065935 X *£0.65*

EUROPEAN COMMUNITIES

The European Communities (Definition of Treaties) (Europe Agreement establishing an Association between the European Communities and their Member States, and the Republic of Slovenia) Order 1998 No. 1062. Enabling power: *European Communities Act 1972, s. 1 (3).* Issued: 30.04.1998. Made: 22.04.1998. Coming into force: In acc.with art. 1. Effect: None. Territorial extent & classification: E/W/S/NI. General. – 2p. – 0 11 065956 2 *£0.65*

The European Communities (Definition of Treaties) (Partnership and Co-operation Agreement between the European Communities and their Member States and the Republic of Uzbekistan) Order 1998 No.1063. Enabling power: *European Communities Act 1972, s. 1 (3).* Issued: 30.04.1998. Made: 22.04.1998. Coming into force: In acc.with art. 1. Effect: None. Territorial extent & classification: E/W/S/NI. General. – 2p. – 0 11 065951 1 *£0.65*

The European Communities (Definition of Treaties) (Partnership and Co-operation Agreement between the European Communities and their Member States and Georgia) Order 1998 No. 1059. Enabling power: *European Communities Act 1972, s. 1 (3).* Issued: 30.04.1998. Made: 22.04.1998. Coming into force: In acc.with art. 1. Effect: None. Territorial extent & classification: E/W/S/NI. General. – 2p. – 0 11 065952 X *£0.65*

The European Communities (Definition of Treaties) (Partnership and Co-operation Agreement between the European Communities and their Member States and the Republic of Armenia) Order 1998 No.1060. Enabling power: *European Communities Act 1972, s. 1 (3).* Issued: 30.04.1998. Made: 22.04.1998. Coming into force: In acc.with art. 1. Effect: None. Territorial extent & classification: E/W/S/NI. General. – 2p. – 0 11 065953 8 *£0.65*

Prices/availability are liable to change without notice

The European Communities (Definition of Treaties) (Partnership and Co-operation Agreement between the European Communities and their Member States and the Republic of Azerbaijan) Order 1998 No.1061. Enabling power: *European Communities Act 1972, s. 1 (3).* Issued: 30.04.1998. Made: 22.04.1998. Coming into force: In acc.with art. 1. Effect: None. Territorial extent & classification: E/W/S/NI. General. – 2p. – 0 11 065954 6 £0.65

FIRE SERVICES: SUPERANNUATION

The Fireman's Pension Scheme (Amendment) Order 1998 No. 1010. Enabling power: *Fire Services Act 1947, s. 26 & Superannuation Act 1972, s. 12* Issued: 20.04.1998. Made: 07.04.1998. Laid: 20.04.1998. Coming into force: 11.05.1998. Effect: S.I. 1992/129 amended. Territorial extent & classification: GB. General. – 4p. – 0 11 065908 2 £1.10

FOOD

The Food Safety (Fishery Products and Live Shellfish) (Hygiene) Regulations 1998 No.994. Enabling power: *Food Safety Act 1990, ss. 6 (4), 16 (1), 17 (1), 18 (1) (c), 26 (1) (b) (3), 48 (1), 49 (2), sch. 1, paras. 2 (2), 5 (1) (2), 6 (1), 7 (1)* Issued: 20.04.1998. Made: 06.04.1998. Laid: 08.04.1998. Coming into force: 29.04.1998. Effect: S.I. 1995/1763; 1996/3124 amended & S.I. 1992/1507, 1508, 3163, 3164, 3165; 1994/2782, 2783; 1996/1547 revoked. Territorial extent & classification: E/W/S. General. – Implements EC DIR 91/492, 493; 92/48; 95/71; 96/43. – With correction slip, dated May 1998 (which replaces one issued in April). – 64p. – 0 11 065920 1 £8.10

FRIENDLY SOCIETIES

The Friendly Societies (General Charge and Fees) Regulations 1998 No. 673. Enabling power: *Friendly Societies Act 1974, s. 104 (1) & Friendly Societies Act 1992, ss. 2 (2) (4), 114 (2).* Issued: 15.04.1998. Made: 11.03.1998. Laid: 11.03.1998. Coming into force: 01.04.1998. Effect: None. Territorial extent & classification: E/W/S/NI. General. – 8p. – 0 11 065902 3 £1.95

HARBOURS, DOCKS, PIERS AND FERRIES

The Exmouth Docks Harbour Revision Order 1998 No. 980. Enabling power: *Harbours Act 1964, s. 14* Issued: 16.04.1998. Made: 20.03.1998. Coming into force: 10.04.1998. Effect: 1864 c. cccxix amended & S.R.& O. 1947/681 repealed. Territorial extent & classification: E. Local. – 4p. – 0 11 065906 6 £1.10

The Port of Birkenhead Harbour Empowerment Order 1998 No. 1016. Enabling power: *Harbours Act 1964, s. 16 (d)* Issued: 24.04.1998. Made: 06.04.1998. Coming into force: 22.04.1998. Effect: None. Territorial extent & classification: E. Local. – 12p. – 0 11 065921 X £2.80

HIGHWAYS, ENGLAND AND WALES

The Northamptonshire County Council (A45 Nene Valley Way Widening) (Bridge Over the River Nene) Scheme 1997 Confirmation Instrument 1998 No. 904. Enabling power: *Highways Act 1980, s. 106 (3)* Issued: 07.04.1998. Made: 23.03.1998. Coming into force: In accord. with art. 1. Effect: None. Territorial extent & classification: E/W. Local. – 6p. – 0 11 065873 6 £1.55

The Street Works (Inspection Fees) (Amendment) Regulations 1998 No. 978. Enabling power: *New Roads and Street Works Act 1991, s. 75* Issued: 16.04.1998. Made: 07.04.1998. Laid: 08.04.1998. Coming into force: 01.05.1998. Effect: S.I. 1992/1688 amended. Territorial extent & classification: E/W. General. – 2p. – 0 11 065914 7 £0.65

The Tyne Tunnel (Revision of Tolls and Traffic Classification) Order 1997 No. 18. Enabling power: *Tyne and Wear Act 1976, s. 13.* Made: 08.01.1998. Coming into force: 08.01.1998. Effect: S.I. 1993/26 revoked. – *Unpublished*

HOUSING, NORTHERN IRELAND

The Housing Accommodation and Homelessness (Persons Subject to Immigration Control) (Northern Ireland) Order 1998 No. 1004. Enabling power: *Asylum and Immigration Act 1996, s. 9* Issued: 22.04.1998. Made: 07.04.1998. Laid: 08.04.1998. Coming into force: 01.05.1998. Effect: S.I. 1996/3274 revoked. Territorial extent & classification: NI. General. – 4p. – 0 11 065926 0 £1.10

HOUSING, SCOTLAND

The Housing Support Grant (Scotland) Order 1998 No. 874 (S. 44). Enabling power: *Housing (Scotland) Act 1987, ss. 191, 192* Issued: 16.04.1998. Made: 17.03.1998. Coming into force: 01.04.1998. Effect: None. Territorial extent & classification: S. General. – 6p. – 0 11 055758 1 £1.55

The Housing Support Grant (Scotland) Variation Order 1998 No. 873 (S. 43). Enabling power: *Housing (Scotland) Act 1987, s. 193 (4) (5)* Issued: 16.04.1998. Made: 17.03.1998. Coming into force: 18.03.1998. Effect: S.I. 1997/940 amended. Territorial extent & classification: S. General. – 2p. – 0 11 055759 X £0.65

IMMIGRATION

The Immigration (Transit Visa) (Amendment No. 2) Order 1998 No. 1014. Enabling power: *Immigration (Carriers' Liability) Act 1987, s. 1A (1) (2)* Issued: 22.04.1998. Made: 07.04.1998. Laid: 08.04.1998. Coming into force: 10.04.1998. Effect: S.I. 1993/1678 amended & S.I. 1995/2621; 1996/2065 revoked. Territorial extent & classification: UK. General. – 2p. – 0 11 065930 9 £0.65

Prices/availability are liable to change without notice

INDUSTRIAL AND PROVIDENT SOCIETIES

The Industrial and Provident Societies (Amendment of Fees) Regulations 1998 No. 676. Enabling power: *Industrial and Provident Societies Act 1965, ss. 70(1), 71(1) & Industrial and Provident Societies Act 1967, s. 7(2)* Issued: 06.04.1998. Made: 11.03.1998. Laid: 11.03.1998. Coming into force: 01.04.1998. Effect: S.I. 1965/1995 amended. Territorial extent & classification: E/W/S/NI. General. – 6p. – 0 11 065869 8 *£1.55*

The Industrial and Provident Societies (Credit Unions) (Amendment of Fees) Regulations 1998 No. 672. Enabling power: *Industrial and Provident Societies Act 1965, ss. 70(1), 71(1) & Credit Unions Act 1979, s. 31(2)* Issued: 06.04.1998. Made: 11.03.1998. Laid: 11.03.1998. Coming into force: 01.04.1998. Effect: S.I. 1979/937 amended. Territorial extent & classification: E/W/S/NI. General. – 4p. – 0 11 065867 1 *£1.10*

LEGAL AID AND ADVICE, ENGLAND AND WALES

The Legal Aid (Mediation in Family Matters) (Amendment) Regulations 1998 No. 900. Enabling power: *Legal Aid Act 1988, s. 13B (2), 34, 43* Issued: 08.04.1998. Made: 26.03.1998. Laid: 27.03.1998. Coming into force: 20.04.1998. Effect: S.I. 1997/1078 amended. Territorial extent & classification: E/W. General. – 2p. – 0 11 065883 3 *£0.65*

LEGAL AID AND ADVICE, SCOTLAND

The Advice and Assistance (Assistance by Way of Representation) (Scotland) Amendment Regulations 1998 No. 972 (S. 55). Enabling power: *Legal Aid (Scotland) Act 1986, ss. 9, 37(1)* Issued: 27.04.1998. Made: 02.04.1998. Coming into force: 06.04.1998. Effect: S.I. 1997/3070 amended. Territorial extent & classification: S. General. – 2p. – 0 11 055765 4 *£0.65*

The Advice and Assistance (Financial Conditions) (Scotland) Regulations 1998 No. 971 (S. 54). Enabling power: *Legal Aid (Scotland) Act 1986, ss. 11(2), 36(2)(b), 37(1)* Issued: 22.04.1998. Made: 02.04.1998. Coming into force: 06.04.1998. Effect: S.I. 1997/1113 revoked with savings. Territorial extent & classification: S. General. – 4p. – 0 11 055767 0 *£1.10*

The Advice and Assistance (Scotland) Amendment Regulations 1998 No. 724 (S. 38). Enabling power: *Legal Aid (Scotland) Act 1986, ss. 12(3), 33(2)(b)(3)(b)(f), 36(1), 37(1)(3), 42* Issued: 08.04.1998. Made: 11.03.1998. Laid: 16.03.1998. Coming into force: 06.04.1998. Effect: S.I. 1996/2447 amended. Territorial extent & classification: S. General. – 4p. – 0 11 055752 2 *£1.10*

The Civil Legal Aid (Financial Conditions) (Scotland) Regulations 1998 No. 970 (S. 53). Enabling power: *Legal Aid (Scotland) Act 1986, s. 36(1)(2)(b)* Issued: 22.04.1998. Made: 02.04.1998. Coming into force: 06.04.1998. Effect: S.I. 1997/1112 revoked with savings. Territorial extent & classification: S. General. – 2p. – 0 11 055766 2 *£0.65*

The Civil Legal Aid (Scotland) Amendment Regulations 1998 No. 725 (S. 39). Enabling power: *Legal Aid (Scotland) Act 1986, ss. 36(1)(2)(a)(g), 37(1)(3), 42* Issued: 08.04.1998. Made: 11.03.1998. Laid: 16.03.1998. Coming into force: 06.04.1998. Effect: S.I. 1996/2444 amended. Territorial extent & classification: S. General. – 4p. – 0 11 055751 4 *£1.10*

The Criminal Legal Aid (Scotland) (Prescribed Proceedings) Amendment Regulations 1998 No.969 (S. 52). Enabling power: *Legal Aid (Scotland) Act 1986, s. 21(2)* Issued: 24.04.1998. Made: 02.04.1998. Coming into force: 06.04.1998. Effect: S.I. 1997/3069 amended. Territorial extent & classification: S. General. – 2p. – 0 11 055764 6 *£0.65*

LEGAL SERVICES

The Institute of Legal Executives Order 1998 No. 1077. Enabling power: *Courts and Legal Services Act 1990, s. 29(2).* Issued: 30.04.1998. Made: 22.04.1998. Coming into force: 23.04.1998. Effect: None. Territorial extent & classification: E/W. General. – 2p. – 0 11 065957 0 *£0.65*

The Legal Services Ombudsman (Jurisdiction) (Amendment) Order 1998 No. 935. Enabling power: *Courts and Legal Services Act 1990, s. 22(7)* Issued: 29.04.1998. Made: 31.03.1998. Laid: 01.04.1998. Coming into force: 23.04.1998. Effect: S.I. 1990/2485 amended. Territorial extent & classification: E/W. General. – 2p. – 0 11 065945 7 *£0.65*

LOCAL GOVERNMENT, ENGLAND AND WALES

The Isle of Wight (Parishes) Order 1998 No. 324. Enabling power: *Local Government and Rating Act 1997, ss. 14, 23.* Made: 13.02.1998. Coming into force: 14.02.1998., 01.04.1998., 07.05.1998. In acc.with art.1. Effect: None. – *Unpublished*

The Local Authorities (Goods and Services) (Public Bodies) (No. 3) Order 1998 No.1123. Enabling power: *Local Authorities (Goods and Services) Act 1970, s. 1(5)* Issued: 30.04.1998. Made: 22.04.1998. Laid: 30.04.1998. Coming into forcve: 21.05.1998. Effect: None. Territorial extent & classification: E/W. General. – 2p. – 0 11 065971 6 *£0.65*

The Local Authorities (Transport Charges) Regulations 1998 No. 948. Enabling power: *Local Government and Housing Act 1989, ss. 150, 152(5)* Issued: 09.04.1998. Made: 31.03.1998. Coming into force: 28.04.1998. Effect: None. Supersedes draft SI ISBN 0110654390 issued 09.02.1998. Territorial extent & classification: E/W. General. – 8p. – 0 11 065885 X *£1.95*

Prices/availability are liable to change without notice

The Local Government Staff Commission (England) (Winding Up) Order 1998 No. 898. Enabling power: *Local Government Act 1992, s. 23 (1) (4)* Issued: 06.04.1998. Made: 24.03.1998. Laid: 06.04.1998. Coming into force: 12.05.1999. Effect: S.I. 1993/1098 revoked. Territorial extent & classification: E/W. General. – 2p. – 0 11 065860 4 £0.65

The National Crime Squad Service Authority (Members' Interests) Regulations 1998 No.1003. Enabling power: *Local Government and Housing Act 1989, ss. 19 (1) (4) (b) (6), 190 (1).* Issued: 15.04.1998. Made: 07.04.1998. Laid: 08.04.1998. Coming into force: 01.05.1998. Effect: S.I. 1992/618 amended. Territorial extent & classification: E/W. General. – 2p. – 0 11 065916 3 £0.65

The National Crime Squad Service Authority (Standing Orders) Regulations 1998 No.1002. Enabling power: *Local Government and Housing Act 1989, ss. 20, 190 (1).* Issued: 15.04.1998. Made: 07.04.1998. Laid: 08.04.1998. Coming into force: 01.05.1998. Effect: None. Territorial extent & classification: E/W. General. – 2p. – 0 11 065915 5 £0.65

The Public Bodies (Admission to Meetings) (National Health Service Trusts) Order 1997 No.2763. Enabling power: *Public Bodies (Admission to Meetings) Act 1960, s. 2 (3).* Issued: 17.04.1998. Made: 20.11.1997. Laid: 20.11.1997. Coming into force: 06.02.1998. Effect: 1960 c. 67 amended. Territorial extent & classification: E/W/S. General. – Supersedes SI of same number 1997/2763 but different ISBN - 0110651618 issued on 27.11.1997. – 2p. – 0 11 065905 8 £0.65

The Public Entertainments Licences (Drug Misuse) Act 1997 (Commencement and Transitional Provisions) Order 1998 No. 1009 (C. 24). Enabling power: *Public Entertainments Licences (Drug Misuse) Act 1997, s. 4 (2) (3). Bringing various provisoins of the 1997 act into operation on 01.05.1998* Issued: 16.04.1998. Made: 06.04.1998. Effect: None. Territorial extent & classification: E/W. General. – 2p. – 0 11 065907 4 £0.65

LOCAL GOVERNMENT, SCOTLAND

The Public Bodies (Admission to Meetings) (National Health Service Trusts) Order 1997 No.2763. Enabling power: *Public Bodies (Admission to Meetings) Act 1960, s. 2 (3).* Issued: 17.04.1998. Made: 20.11.1997. Laid: 20.11.1997. Coming into force: 06.02.1998. Effect: 1960 c. 67 amended. Territorial extent & classification: E/W/S. General. – Supersedes SI of same number 1997/2763 but different ISBN - 0110651618 issued on 27.11.1997. – 2p. – 0 11 065905 8 £0.65

MARINE POLLUTION

The Merchant Shipping (Oil Pollution Preparedness, Response and Co-operation Convention) Regulations 1998 No. 1056. Enabling power: *S.I. 1997/2567, art. 2.* Issued: 23.04.1998. Made: 16.04.1998. Laid: 23.04.1998. Coming into force: 15.05.1998. Effect: None. Territorial extent & classification: E/W/S/NI. General. – 6p. – 0 11 065937 6 £1.55

MEDICINES

The Medicines (Exemptions for Merchants in Veterinary Drugs)Order 1998 No. 1044. Enabling power: *Medicines Act 1968, ss. 57 (1) (2) (2A), 129 (4) & European Communities Act 1972, s. 2 (2)* Issued: 27.04.1998. Made: 09.04.1998. Laid: 15.04.1998. Coming into force: 06.05.1998. Effect: S.I. 1992/33, 3081; 1994/599, 3169; 1995/3193; 1996/3034; 1997/2892 revoked. Territorial extent & classification: E/W/S/NI. General. – Implements provisions of DIR 81/851/EEC on the approximation of the laws of Member States relating to veterinary medicinal products. – 8p. – 0 11 065940 6 £1.95

The Medicines (Sale or Supply) (Miscellaneous Provisions) Amendment Regulations 1998 No.1045. Enabling power: *Medicines Act 1968, ss. 66 (1), 67 (6), 108 (4) (7), 129 (1)* Issued: 27.04.1998. Made: 09.04.1998. Laid: 15.04.1998. Coming into force: 06.05.1998. Effect: S.I. 1980/1923 amended. Territorial extent & classification: E/W/S/NI. General. – 4p. – 0 11 065939 2 £1.10

MERCHANT SHIPPING

The Merchant Shipping (Crew Accommodation) (Fishing Vessels) (Amendment) Regulations 1998 No.929. Enabling power: *Merchant Shipping Act 1995, s. 121, 307 & European Communities Act 1972, s. 2 (2)* Issued: 07.04.1998. Made: 30.03.1998. Laid: 07.04.1998. Coming into force: 01.05.1998. Effect: S.I. 1975/2220 amended. Territorial extent & classification: E/W/S/NI. General. – 6p. – 0 11 065874 4 £1.55

The Merchant Shipping (Oil Pollution) (Pitcairn) (Amendment) Order 1998 No. 1067. Enabling power: *Merchant Shipping Act 1995, s. 315 (2)* Issued: 30.04.1998. Made: 22.04.1998. Coming into force: 23.04.1998. Effect: S.I. 1997/2585 amended. Territorial extent & classification: General. – 2p. – 0 11 065959 7 £0.65

The Merchant Shipping (Oil Pollution) (Sovereign Base Areas) (Amendment) Order 1998 No.1068. Enabling power: *Merchant Shipping Act 1995, s. 315 (2)* Issued: 30.04.1998. Made: 22.04.1998. Coming into force: 23.04.1998. Effect: S.I. 1997/2587 amended. Territorial extent & classification: General. – 2p. – 0 11 065958 9 £0.65

MERCHANT SHIPPING: MASTERS AND SEAMEN

The Fishing Vessels (Certification of Deck Officers and Engineer Officers) (Amendment) Regulations 1998 No. 1013. Enabling power: *Merchant Shipping Act 1995, s. 47.* Issued: 15.04.1998. Made: 04.04.1998. Laid: 15.04.1998. Coming into force: 08.05.1998. Effect: S.I. 1984/1115 amended. Territorial extent & classification: E/W/S/NI. General. – 2p. – 0 11 065913 9 £0.65

Prices/availability are liable to change without notice

MERCHANT SHIPPING: SAFETY

The Fishing Vessels (Life-Saving Appliances) (Amendment) Regulations 1998 No. 927. Enabling power: *Merchant Shipping Act 1995, s. 85(1)(a)(3), 86(1)* Issued: 07.04.1998. Made: 30.03.1998. Laid: 07.04.1998. Coming into force: 01.05.1998. Effect: S.I. 1988/38 amended. Territorial extent & classification: E/W/S/NI. General. – 4p. – 0 11 065876 0 £1.10

The Fishing Vessels (Safety Provisions) (Amendment) Rules 1998 No. 928. Enabling power: *Merchant Shipping Act 1995, s. 121, 307 & European Communities Act 1972, s. 2 (2)* Issued: 07.04.1998. Made: 30.03.1998. Laid: 07.04.1998. Coming into force: 01.05.1998. Effect: S.I. 1975/330 amended. Territorial extent & classification: E/W/S/NI. General. – Implements parts of EC DIR 93/103. – 6p. – 0 11 065875 2 £1.55

The Merchant Shipping (Fire Protection:Large Ships) Regulations 1998 No. 1012. Enabling power: *Merchant Shipping Act 1995, ss. 85(1)(a)(b)(c)(3)(5) to (7), 86(1)* Issued: 20.04.1998. Made: 07.04.1998. Laid: 20.04.1998. Coming into force: 11.05.1998. Effect: S.I. 1980/544; 1981/574; 1984/1218; 1985/1193, 1194, 1218; 1986/1070, 1248; 1992/2360; 1993/3161, 3162, 3163, 3164 revoked. Territorial extent & classification: E/W/S/NI. General. – 68p. – 0 11 065910 4 £8.10

The Merchant Shipping (Fire Protection:Small Ships) Regulations 1998 No. 1011. Enabling power: *Merchant Shipping Act 1995, ss. 85(1)(a)(b)(c)(3)(5) to (7), 86(1)* Issued: 20.04.1998. Made: 07.04.1998. Laid: 20.04.1998. Coming into force: 11.05.1998. Effect: None. Territorial extent & classification: E/W/S/NI. General. – 28p. – 0 11 065909 0 £4.70

METROPOLITAN AND CITY POLICE DISTRICTS

The London Cab Order 1998 No. 1043. Enabling power: *Metropolitan Public Carriage Act 1869, s. 9, London Cab and Stage Carriage Act 1907, s.1, & London Cab Act 1968, s. 1* Issued: 23.04.1998. Made: 04.04.1998. Coming into force: 25.04.1998. Effect: S.R & O 1934/1346 amended. Territorial extent & classification: E. Local. – 2p. – 0 11 065927 9 £0.65

NATIONAL HEALTH SERVICE, ENGLAND AND WALES

The Community Health Care: North Durham National Health Service Trust (Dissolution) Order 1998 No. 822. Enabling power: *National Health Service Act 1977, s. 126 (3)* Issued: 31.03.1998. Made: 19.03.1998. Coming into force: 01.04.1998. Effect: S.I. 1993/2612 revoked. Territorial extent & classification: E/W. General. – 4p. – 0 11 065823 X £1.10

The East London and the City Health Authority (Transfers of Trust Property) Order 1998 No.977. Enabling power: *National Health Service Act 1977, s. 92 (1)*. Issued: 15.04.1998. Made: 06.04.1998. Laid: 07.04.1998. Coming into force: 28.04.1998. Effect: None. Territorial extent & classification: E/W. General. – 2p. – 0 11 065903 1 £0.65

The Lewisham and Guy's Mental Health National Health Service Trust (Transfer of Trust Property) Order 1998 No. 895. Enabling power: *National Health Service Act 1977, s. 92 (1)* Issued: 02.04.1998. Made: 25.03.1998. Laid: 02.04.1998. Coming into force: 23.04.1998. Effect: None. Territorial extent & classification: E/W. General. – 2p. – 0 11 065857 4 £0.65

The Lifespan Health Care Cambridge National Health Service Trust (Establishment) Amendment Order 1998 No. 957. Enabling power: *National Health Service Act 1977, s. 126(3) & National Health Service and Community Care Act 1990, s. 5 (1)* Issued: 09.04.1998. Made: 01.04.1998. Coming into force: 02.04.1998. Effect: S.I. 1992/2571 amended. Territorial extent & classification: E/W. General. – 4p. – 0 11 065891 4 £1.10

The Lincolnshire Ambulance and Health Transport Service National Health Service Trust (Transfer of Trust Property) Order 1998 No. 896. Enabling power: *National Health Service Act 1977, s. 92 (1)* Issued: 02.04.1998. Made: 25.03.1998. Laid: 02.04.1998. Coming into force: 23.04.1998. Effect: None. Territorial extent & classification: E/W. General. – 2p. – 0 11 065858 2 £0.65

The Special Trustees for the Middlesex Hospital (Transfer of Trust Property) Order 1998 No.1104. Enabling power: *National Health Service Act 1977, s. 92 (1)* Issued: 28.04.1998. Made: 21.04.1998. Laid: 23.04.1998. Coming into force: 14.05.1998. Effect: None. Territorial extent & classification: E/W. General. – 2p. – 0 11 065941 4 £0.65

The Special Trustees for University College Hospital (Transfer of Trust Property) Order 1998 No. 897. Enabling power: *National Health Service Act 1977, s. 92 (1)* Issued: 02.04.1998. Made: 25.03.1998. Laid: 06.04.1998. Coming into force: 27.04.1998. Effect: None. Territorial extent & classification: E/W,. General. – 2p. – 0 11 065859 0 £0.65

NATIONAL HEALTH SERVICE, SCOTLAND

The Hairmyres and Stonehouse Hospitals National Health Service Trust (Establishment) Amendment Order 1998 No. 804 (S. 41). Enabling power: *National Health Service Trust (Scotland) Act 1978, s. 12A (1), sch. 7A, paras. 1, 3(1)(b)* Issued: 08.04.1998. Made: 13.03.1998. Coming into force: 18.03.1998. Effect: S.I. 1993/2928 amended. Territorial extent & classification: S. General. – 2p. – 0 11 055750 6 £0.65

The Law Hospital National Health Service Trust (Establishment) Amendment Order 1998 No.926 (S. 50). Enabling power: *National Health Service (Scotland) Act 1978, s. 12A(1), sch. 7A, paras. 1, 3(1)(b)* Issued: 22.04.1998. Made: 26.03.1998. Coming into force: 01.04.1998. Effect: S.I. 1993/2929 amended. Territorial extent & classification: S. General. – 2p. – 0 11 055762 X £0.65

Prices/availability are liable to change without notice

186 *PENSIONS*

The Monklands and Bellshill Hospitals National Health Service Trust (Establishment) (Change of Name and Amendment) Order 1998 No. 922 (S. 48). Enabling power: *National Health Service (Scotland) Act 1978, s. 12A (1), sch. 7A, paras. 1, 3 (1) (a) (b)* Issued: 22.04.1998. Made: 26.03.1998. Coming into force: 01.04.1998. Effect: S.I. 1993/3308 amended. Territorial extent & classification: S. General. – 2p. – 0 11 055760 3 *£0.65*

The National Health Service (Choice of Medical Practitioner) (Scotland) Regulations 1998 No.659 (S. 29). Enabling power: *National Health Service (Scotland) Act 1978, ss. 17F (1) (2) (5), 19, 105 (7)* Issued: 06.04.1998. Made: 09.03.1998. Laid: 11.03.1998. Coming into force: 01.04.1999. Effect: S.I. 1995/416 amended. Territorial extent & classification: S. General. – 8p. – 0 11 055738 7 *£1.95*

The National Health Service (Fund-holding Practices) (Scotland) Amendment Regulations 1998 No. 658 (S. 28). Enabling power: *National Health Service (Scotland) Act 1978, ss. 2 (5), 87A (4), 87B (5), 87C (1) to (4), 105 (7), 106 (a), 108 (1)* Issued: 06.04.1998. Made: 09.03.1998. Laid: 11.03.1998. Coming into force: 01.04.1998. Effect: S.I. 1997/1014 amended. Territorial extent & classification: S. General. – 6p. – 0 11 055739 5 *£1.55*

The National Health Service (General Medical Services) (Scotland) Amendment (No. 2) Regulations 1998 No. 660 (S. 30). Enabling power: *National Health Service (Scotland) Act 1978, ss. 2 (5), 19, 105 (7), 108 (1)* Issued: 02.04.1998. Made: 09.03.1998. Laid: 11.03.1998. Coming into force: 01.04.1998. Effect: S.I. 1995/416 amended. Territorial extent & classification: S. General. – 8p. – 0 11 055741 7 *£1.95*

The National Health Service (Service Committees and Tribunal) (Scotland) Amendment Regulations 1998 No. 657 (S. 27). Enabling power: *National Health Service (Scotland) Act 1978, ss. 19 (2), 32, 105 (7), 106 (a) & National Health Service (Primary Care) Act 1997, ss. 39(1), 40(2), sch.1, paras. 3(4)(5)* Issued: 02.04.1998. Made: 09.03.1998. Laid: 11.03.1998. Coming into force: 01.04.1998. Effect: S.I. 1992/434 amended. Territorial extent & classification: S. General. – 4p. – 0 11 055740 9 *£1.10*

NORTHERN IRELAND

The Northern Ireland Arms Decommissioning Act 1997 (Amnesty Period) Order 1998 No.893. Enabling power: *Northern Ireland Decommissioning Act 1997, s. 2 (2) (b)* Issued: 01.04.1998. Made: 23.03.1998. Coming into force: 24.03.1998. Effect: None. Supersedes draft SI ISBN 0110656210 issued 10.03.1998. Territorial extent & classification: NI. General. – 2p. – 0 11 065850 7 *£0.65*

The Northern Ireland (Entry to Negotiations, etc) Act 1996 (Cessation of Section 3) Order 1998 No. 1127. Enabling power: *Northern Ireland (Entry to Negotiations, etc) Act 1996, s. 7 (3) (4)* Issued: 29.04.1998. Made: 24.04.1998. Coming into force: 25.04.1998. Effect: S.I. 1997/1410 revoked. Territorial extent & classification: NI. General. – Supersedes draft SI ISBN 0110659368 issued on 21.04.1998. – 2p. – 0 11 065974 0 *£0.65*

The Northern Ireland Negotiations (Referendum) Order 1998 No. 1126. Enabling power: *Northern Ireland (Entry to Negotiations, etc.) Act 1996, s. 4(1)* Issued: 29.04.1998. Made: 24.04.1998. Coming into force: 25.04.1998. Effect: None. Territorial extent & classification: NI. General. – Supersedes draft SI ISBN 0110659333 issued on 20.04.1998. – 20p. – 0 11 065973 2 *£3.70*

The Public Processions (Northern Ireland) Act 1998 (Notice of Processions) (Exceptions) Order 1998 No. 956. Enabling power: *Public Processions (Northern Ireland) Act 1998, s. 6 (5) (b)* Issued: 14.04.1998. Made: 01.04.1998. Laid: 06.04.1998. Coming into force: 01.05.1998. Effect: S.I. 1998/583 revoked [before published]. Territorial extent & classification: NI. General. – 2p. – 0 11 065893 0 *£0.65*

NURSES, MIDWIVES AND HEALTH VISITORS

The Nurses, Midwives and Health Visitors (Professional Conduct) (Amendment) Rules 1998 Approval Order 1998 No. 1103. Enabling power: *Nurses, Midwives and Health Visitors Act 1997, s. 19 (5)* Issued: 29.04.1998. Made: 20.04.1998. Coming into force: 18.05.1998. Effect: None. Territorial extent & classification: E/W/S. General. – 4p. – 0 11 065946 5 *£1.10*

OSTEOPATHS

The General Osteopathic Council (Conditional Registration) Rules Order of Council 1998 No.1020. Enabling power: *Osteopaths Act 1993, ss. 4 (2) (e) (10) (11), 6 (3) (g) (l)* Issued: 17.04.1998. Made: 30.03.1998. Coming into force: 01.04.1998. Effect: None. Territorial extent & classification: E/W/S/NI. General. – 4p. – 0 11 065917 1 *£1.10*

The General Osteopathic Council (Constitution and Procedure) Rules Order of Council 1998 No.1019. Enabling power: *Osteopaths Act 1993, ss. 1 (8) (9), 35 (2), sch., paras. 4 (2) (4), 7, 14 (5), 16 (2), 17 (4), 20* Issued: 17.04.1998. Made: 30.03.1998. Coming into force: 01.04.1998. Effect: None. Territorial extent & classification: E/W/S/NI. General. – 6p. – 0 11 065919 8 *£1.55*

The General Osteopathic Council (Transitional Period) (Application for Registration and Fees) Rules Order of Council 1998 No. 1018. Enabling power: *Osteopaths Act 1993, ss. 3 (2) (a) (5), 4 (2) (a) (9)* Issued: 17.04.1998. Made: 30.03.1998. Coming into force: 01.04.1998. Effect: None. Territorial extent & classification: E/W/S/NI. General. – 14p. – 0 11 065918 X *£3.20*

PENSIONS

The Local Government Pension Scheme (Scotland) Regulations 1998 No. 366 (S. 14). Correction slip, dated April 1998. – *Free*

Prices/availability are liable to change without notice

The Social Security (Minimum Contributions to Appropriate Personal Pension Schemes) Order 1998 No. 944.
Enabling power: *Pension Schemes Act 1993, s. 45A* Issued: 03.04.1998. Coming into force: 06.04.1998. Effect: S.I. 1996/1056 amended. Supersedes draft SI ISBN 0110655958 issued on 04.03.1998. Territorial extent & classification: E/W/S. General. –4p. –0 11 065878 7 *£1.10*

The Social Security (Reduced Rates of Class 1 Contributions, and Rebates) (Money Purchase Contracted-out Schemes) Order 1998 No. 945. Enabling power: *Pension Schemes Act 1993, s. 42B* Issued: 03.04.1998. Coming into force: 06.04.1998. Effect: S.I. 1996/1055 amended. Supersedes draft SI ISBN 0110655966 issued 04.03.1998. Territorial extent & classification: E/W/S. General. –4p. –0 11 065879 5 *£1.10*

PETROLEUM

The Offshore Petroleum Production and Pipe-lines (Assessment of Environmental Effects) Regulations 1998 No. 968. Enabling power: *European Communities Act 1972, s. 2 (2)* Issued: 30.04.1998. Made: 04.04.1998. Laid: 07.04.1998. Coming into force: 30.04.1998. Effect: None. Territorial extent & classification: E/W/S/NI. General. – Implements EC DIR 85/337. – 16p. –0 11 065961 9 *£3.20*

PIPE-LINES

The Offshore Petroleum Production and Pipe-lines (Assessment of Environmental Effects) Regulations 1998 No. 968. Enabling power: *European Communities Act 1972, s. 2 (2)* Issued: 30.04.1998. Made: 04.04.1998. Laid: 07.04.1998. Coming into force: 30.04.1998. Effect: None. Territorial extent & classification: E/W/S/NI. General. – Implements EC DIR 85/337. – 16p. –0 11 065961 9 *£3.20*

POLICE

The National Crime Squad Service Authority (Members' Interests) Regulations 1998 No.1003. Enabling power: *Local Government and Housing Act 1989, ss. 19 (1) (4) (b) (6), 190 (1).* Issued: 15.04.1998. Made: 07.04.1998. Laid: 08.04.1998. Coming into force: 01.05.1998. Effect: S.I. 1992/618 amended. Territorial extent & classification: E/W. General. –2p. –0 11 065916 3 *£0.65*

The National Crime Squad Service Authority (Standing Orders) Regulations 1998 No.1002. Enabling power: *Local Government and Housing Act 1989, ss. 20, 190 (1).* Issued: 15.04.1998. Made: 07.04.1998. Laid: 08.04.1998. Coming into force: 01.05.1998. Effect: None. Territorial extent & classification: E/W. General. –2p. –0 11 065915 5 *£0.65*

The Police Act 1997 (Provisions in relation to the NCIS Service Authority) Order 1998 No.633. Correction slip dated April 1998. – *Free*

The Police Grant (No. 2) (Scotland) Order 1998 No. 891 (S. 46). Enabling power: *Police (Scotland) Act 1967, s. 32 (3) (5)* Issued: 09.04.1998. Made: 23.03.1998. Laid: 25.03.1998. Coming into force: 15.04.1998. Effect: None. Territorial extent & classification: S. General. –4p. –0 11 055756 5 *£1.10*

The Police Grant (Scotland) Order 1998 No. 611 (S. 22). Enabling power: *Police (Scotland) Act 1967, s. 32 (3)* Issued: 02.04.1998. Made: 11.03.1998. Coming into force: 31.03.1998. Effect: None. Territorial extent & classification: S. General. –2p. –0 11 055745 X *£1.10*

PUBLIC HEALTH, ENGLAND AND WALES

The Residential Care Homes and the Nursing Homes and Mental Nursing Homes (Amendment) Regulations 1998 No. 902. Enabling power: *Residential Homes Act 1984, ss. 5 (1), 8, 23 (2) (b), 27, 56 (4)* Issued: 07.04.1998. Made: 27.03.1998. Laid: 08.04.1998. Coming into force: 01.05.1998. Effect: S.I. 1984/1345, 1578 amended & S.I. 1990/2164, 1992/2007 revoked. Territorial extent & classification: E/W. General. – 2p. 0 11 065877 9 *£0.65*

PUBLIC RECORDS

The Public Record Office (Fees) Regulations 1998 No. 599. Enabling power: *Public Records Act 1958, s. 2 (5)* Issued: 06.04.1998. Made: 06.03.1998. Coming into force: 01.04.1998. Effect: S.I. 1997/400 revoked. Territorial extent & classification: E/W. General. –6p. –0 11 065866 3 *£1.55*

RATING AND VALUATION

The Railways (Rateable Values) (Scotland) Order 1998 No. 947 (S. 51). Enabling power: *Local Government (Scotland) Act 1975, ss. 6, 35, 37 (1)* Issued: 16.04.1998. Made: 30.03.1998. Coming into force: 31.03.1998. Effect: 1956 c. 60; 1975 c. 30 amended & S.I. 1995/930 revoked. Territorial extent & classification: S. General. –6p. –0 11 055763 8 *£1.55*

REFERENDUM

The Greater London Authority (Referendum Arrangements) Order 1998 No. 746. Enabling power: *Greater London Authority (Referendum) Act 1998, s. 4* Issued: 01.04.1998. Made: 18.03.1998. Coming into force: 19.03.1998. Effect: 1983 c. 2; 1985 c. 50; S.I. 1986/1081 amended. Territorial extent & classification: E/W. General. – Supersedes draft SI ISBN 0110657071 issued on 13.03.1998. –28p. –0 11 065777 2 *£4.70*

Prices/availability are liable to change without notice

ROADS AND BRIDGES, SCOTLAND

The A75 Trunk Road (The Glen Improvement) (Variation) Order 1998 No. 21. Enabling power: *Roads (Scotland) Act 1984, ss. 5(2), 143(1), 145(1).* Made: 07.01.1998. Coming into force: 16.01.1998. Effect: S.I. 1997/1685 amended. *– Unpublished*

The A86 Trunk Road (Rubha Na Magach to Aberarder) Order 1998 No. 339. Enabling power: *Roads (Scotland) Act 1984, ss. 5(2), 12(1), 143(1).* Made: 18.02.1998. Coming into force: 27.02.1998. Effect: None. *– Unpublished*

The Road Works (Inspection Fees) (Scotland) Amendment Regulations 1998 No. 1029 (S. 58). Enabling power: *New Roads and Street Works Act 1991, ss. 134, 163 (1)* Issued: 23.04.1998. Made: 07.04.1998. Laid: 09.04.1998. Coming into force: 01.05.1998. Effect: S.I. 1992/1676 amended. Territorial extent & classification: S. General. – 2p. – 0 11 055770 0 *£0.65*

ROADS AND BRIDGES, SCOTLAND: SPECIAL ROADS

The Glasgow-Carlisle Special Road A74(M) (Paddy's Rickle Bridge-Harthope Special Road) (Variation) Scheme 1998 No. 365. Enabling power: *Roads (Scotland) Act 1984, ss. 7, 143 (1), 145.* Made: 20.02.1998. Coming into force: 27.02.1998. Effect: None. *– Unpublished*

ROAD TRAFFIC

The A41 Trunk Road (Camden) (Temporary Prohibition of Traffic) (No. 2) Order 1998 No. 866. Enabling power: *Road Traffic Regulation Act 1984, s. 14* Issued: 14.04.1998. Made: 20.03.1998. Coming into force: 06.04.1998. Effect: None. Territorial extent & classification: E. Local. – 2p. – 0 11 065899 X *£0.65*

The A41 Trunk Road (Westminster) Red Route (No. 2) Traffic Order 1998 No. 938. Enabling power: *Road Traffic Regulation Act 1984, s. 6* Issued: 27.04.1998. Made: 30.03.1998. Coming into force: 10.04.1998. Effect: S.I. 1996/2688 revoked. Territorial extent & classification: E. Local. – 8p. – 0 11 065938 4 *£1.95*

The A205 Trunk Road (Greenwich) Red Route Experimental Traffic Order 1997 Variation Order 1998 No. 979. Enabling power: *Road Traffic Regulation Act 1984, ss. 9, 10* Issued: 22.04.1998. Made: 06.04.1998. Coming into force: 17.04.1998. Effect: S.I. 1997/139 amended. Territorial extent & classification: E. Local. – 2p. – 0 11 065932 5 *£0.65*

The A205 Trunk Road (Lambeth) Red Route (Prohibition of Traffic) Experimental Traffic Order 1998 No. 883. Enabling power: *Road Traffic Regulation Act 1984, s. 9* Issued: 14.04.1998. Made: 20.03.1998. Coming into force: 06.04.1998. Effect: None. Territorial extent & classification: E. Local. – 2p. – 0 11 065897 3 *£0.65*

The A205 Trunk Road (Lewisham) Red Route (Bus Lanes) Traffic Order 1998 No. 884. Enabling power: *Road Traffic Regulation Act 1984, s. 6* Issued: 14.04.1998. Made: 20.03.1998. Coming into force: 03.04.1998. Effect: S.I. 1997/555 revoked in so far as its provisions relate to any length of road specified in the schedule. Territorial extent & classification: E. Local. – 4p. – 0 11 065898 1 *£1.10*

The London Borough of Haringey (Trunk Roads) Red Route (Bus Lanes) Traffic Order 1997 Variation Order 1998 No. 867. Enabling power: *Road Traffic Regulation Act 1984, s. 6* Issued: 07.04.1998. Made: 20.03.1998. Coming into force: 03.04.1998. Effect: S.I. 1997/449 amended. Territorial extent & classification: E/W. Local. – 2p. – 0 11 065880 9 *£0.65*

The Pelican and Puffin Pedestrian Crossings General (Amendment) Directions 1998 No. 901. Enabling power: *Road Traffic Regulation Act 1984, s. 65 (1)* Issued: 03.04.1998. Made: 25.03.1998. Coming into force: 01.04.1998. Effect: S.I. 1997/2400 amended. This SI has been made in consequence of a defect in SI 1997/2400 and is being sent free of charge to all known recipients of that SI. ONLY those already possessing original SI ISBN 0110649656 require this otherwise the version including both the original and amendment (ISBN 0110658647) is required. Territorial extent & classification: E/W/S. General. – 2p. – 0 11 065863 9 *£0.65*

The Road Traffic Act 1991 (Commencement No. 15 and Transitional Provisions) Order 1998 No. 967 (C. 22). Enabling power: *Road Traffic Act 1991, s. 84. Bringing into operation various provisions of the 1991 act on 10.04.1998.* Issued: 14.04.1998. Made: 31.03.1998. Effect: S.I. 1993/1461, 2229, 2803, 3238; 1994/81, 1482, 1484 amended. Territorial extent & classification: E/W/S. General. – 2p. – 0 11 065896 5 *£0.65*

The Road Vehicles Registration Fee (Amendment) Regulations 1998 No. 995. Enabling power: *Vehicle Excise and Regulation Act 1994, ss. 21 (3), 57.* Issued: 30.04.1998. Made: 07.04.1998. Laid: 08.04.1998. Coming into force: 09.04.1998. Effect: S.I. 1998/572 amended. Territorial extent & classification: E/W/S/NI. General. – This SI has been made in consequence of a defect in SI 1998/572 and is being sent free of charge to all known recipients of that SI. ONLY those already possessing original SI ISBN 0110656644 require this. – 2p. – 0 11 065948 1 *£0.65*

ROAD TRAFFIC: SPEED LIMITS

The A5 Trunk Road (Watling Street, Pattishall, Northamptonshire) (50 mph Speed Limit) Order 1998 No. 145. Enabling power: *Road Traffic Regulation Act 1984, s. 84(1)(a)(2).* Made: 26.01.1998. Coming into force: 09.02.1998. Effect: None. *– Unpublished*

The Gretna-Stranraer Trunk Road (A75) (Restricted Road) (Springholm) (Variation) Order 1998 No. 160. Enabling power: *Road Traffic Regulation Act 1984, ss. 82 (2) (b), 83 (1), 124 (1) (d).* Made: 23.01.1998. Coming into force: 16.02.1998. Effect: S.I. 1988/1705 amended. *– Unpublished*

Prices/availability are liable to change without notice

ROAD TRAFFIC: TRAFFIC REGULATION

The A1 Trunk Road (Carlton on Trent to North Muskham, Nottinghamshire) (Temporary Restriction and Prohibition of Traffic) Order 1998 No. 14. Enabling power: *Road Traffic Regulation Act 1984, s. 14 (1) (a)*. Made: 05.01.1998. Coming into force: 12.01.1998. Effect: None. – *Unpublished*

The A1 Trunk Road (Fairburn to Brotherton) (Temporary Restriction and Prohibition of Traffic) Order 1998 No. 70. Enabling power: *Road Traffic Regulation Act 1984, s. 14 (1) (a)*. Made: 14.01.1998. Coming into force: 16.01.1998. Effect: None. – *Unpublished*

The A1 Trunk Road (Nene Valley Railway to Water Newton, Cambridgeshire) (Temporary Restriction of Traffic) Order 1998 No. 148. Enabling power: *Road Traffic Regulation Act 1984, s. 14 (1) (a)*. Made: 26.01.1998. Coming into force: 02.02.1998. Effect: None. – *Unpublished*

The A1 Trunk Road (North of Black Cat to Wyboston) (Temporary Restriction and Prohibition of Traffic) Order 1998 No. 98. Enabling power: *Road Traffic Regulation Act 1984, s. 14 (1) (a)*. Made: 19.01.1998. Coming into force: 26.01.1998. Effect: None. – *Unpublished*

The A1 Trunk Road (Rainton Crossroads) (Prohibition of U-turns) Order 1998 No. 146. Enabling power: *Road Traffic Regulation Act 1984, ss. 1 (1), 2 (1) (2)*. Made: 29.01.1998. Coming into force: 02.02.1998. Effect: None. – *Unpublished*

The A1 Trunk Road (Upper Street and Islington High Street, Islington) (Temporary Restriction of Traffic) Order 1998 No. 181. Enabling power: *Road Traffic Regulation Act 1984, s. 14 (1) (4) (5) (7)*. Made: 27.01.1998. Coming into force: 01.02.1998. Effect: None. – *Unpublished*

The A1 Trunk Road (Wentbridge to Barnsdale Bar) (Temporary Restriction and Prohibition of Traffic) Order 1998 No. 137. Enabling power: *Road Traffic Regulation Act 1984, s. 14 (1) (a)*. Made: 21.01.1998. Coming into force: 23.01.1998. Effect: None. – *Unpublished*

The A1(M) Motorway and A194(M) Motorway (Burtree Interchange to Whitemare Pool) (Temporary Restriction of Traffic) Order 1998 No. 13. Enabling power: *Road Traffic Regulation Act 1984, s. 14 (1) (a) (c) (7)*. Made: 02.01.1998. Coming into force: 04.01.1998. Effect: None. – *Unpublished*

The A1(M) Motorway (Junction 2 - Northbound Exit Slip Road) (Temporary Prohibition of Traffic) Order 1998 No. 238. Enabling power: *Road Traffic Regulation Act 1984, s. 14 (1) (a)*. Made: 02.02.1998. Coming into force: 07.02.1998. Effect: None. – *Unpublished*

The A1(M) Motorway (Junction 8, Hertfordshire) (Temporary Restriction and Prohibition of Traffic) Order 1998 No. 149. Enabling power: *Road Traffic Regulation Act 1984, s. 14 (1) (a) (7)*. Made: 26.01.1998. Coming into force: 02.02.1998. Effect: None. – *Unpublished*

The A3 Trunk Road (Wisley Interchange) (Closure of a Bus Bay) Order 1998 No. 142. Enabling power: *Road Traffic Regulation Act 1984, ss. 1 (1), 2 (1) (2)*. Made: 26.01.1998. Coming into force: 09.02.1998. Effect: None. – *Unpublished*

The A5 Trunk Road (Cefni Bridge, Anglesey) (Temporary 30mph Speed Limit) Order 1998 No. 74. Enabling power: *Road Traffic Regulation Act 1984, s. 14 (1) (4)*. Made: 02.01.1998. Coming into force: 02.01.1998. Effect: None. – *Unpublished*

The A5 Trunk Road (Cornhill to C54 Junction, Northamptonshire) (Temporary Restriction of Traffic) Order 1998 No. 49. Enabling power: *Road Traffic Regulation Act 1984, s. 14 (1) (a)*. Made: 12.01.1998. Coming into force: 19.01.1998. Effect: None. – *Unpublished*

The A6 Trunk Road (Great Glen to Burton Overy, Leicestershire) (Temporary Speed Restriction) Order 1998 No. 96. Enabling power: *Road Traffic Regulation Act 1984, s. 14 (1) (a)*. Made: 19.01.1998. Coming into force: 26.01.1998. Effect: None. – *Unpublished*

The A8 Trunk Road (East Hamilton Street/Sinclair Street Junction, Greenock) (Temporary Prohibition of Specified Turns) Order 1998 No. 92. Enabling power: *Road Traffic Regulation Act 1984, s. 14 (1) (a)*. Made: 16.01.1998. Coming into force: 26.01.1998. Effect: None. – *Unpublished*

The A14 Trunk Road (Cambridgeshire to Felixstowe) (Temporary Restriction and Prohibition of Traffic) Order 1998 No. 40. Enabling power: *Road Traffic Regulation Act 1984, s. 14 (1) (a)*. Made: 12.01.1998. Coming into force: 19.01.1998. Effect: None. – *Unpublished*

The A20 Trunk Road (Marker Posts 16.60-20.60) (Temporary 50 Miles Per Hour Speed Restriction) Order 1998 No. 34. Enabling power: *Road Traffic Regulation Act 1984, s. 14 (1) (a)*. Made: 12.01.1998. Coming into force: 17.01.1998. Effect: None. – *Unpublished*

The A30 Trunk Road (Camborne Bypass) (Temporary Restriction and Prohibition of Traffic) Order 1998 No. 10. Enabling power: *Road Traffic Regulation Act 1984, s. 14 (1) (a)*. Made: 05.01.1998. Coming into force: 10.01.1998. Effect: None. – *Unpublished*

The A30 Trunk Road (Hawkstor to Colliford) (Temporary 30 Miles Per Hour Speed Restriction) Order 1998 No. 154. Enabling power: *Road Traffic Regulation Act 1984, s. 14 (1) (a)*. Made: 26.01.1998. Coming into force: 31.01.1998. Effect: None. – *Unpublished*

The A30 Trunk Road (Mount Pleasant to Innis Downs) (Temporary 30 Miles Per Hour Speed Restriction) Order 1998 No. 135. Enabling power: *Road Traffic Regulation Act 1984, s. 14 (1) (a)*. Made: 19.01.1998. Coming into force: 24.01.1998. Effect: None. – *Unpublished*

Prices/availability are liable to change without notice

The A30 Trunk Road (Tregoss Moor Bridge) (Temporary Prohibition of Traffic) Order 1998 No.11. Enabling power: *Road Traffic Regulation Act 1984, s. 14(1)(a)* Made: 05.01.1998. Coming into force: 10.01.1998. Effect: None. – *Unpublished*

The A34 Trunk Road (Kings Worthy - Three Maids Hill) (Temporary Restriction and Prohibition of Traffic) Order 1998 No. 91. Enabling power: *Road Traffic Regulation Act 1984, s. 14(1)(a)*. Made: 19.01.1998. Coming into force: 24.01.1998. Effect: None. – *Unpublished*

The A34 Trunk Road (Whitway to Burghclere) (Temporary 50 Miles Per Hour Speed Restriction) Order 1998 No. 144. Enabling power: *Road Traffic Regulation Act 1984, s. 14 (1) (a)*. Made: 26.01.1998. Coming into force: 31.01.1998. Effect: None. – *Unpublished*

The A36 Trunk Road (East Clyffe Layby) (Temporary Prohibition of Traffic) Order 1998 No.39. Enabling power: *Road Traffic Regulation Act 1984, s. 14 (1) (a)*. Made: 09.01.1998. Coming into force: 10.01.1998. Effect: None. – *Unpublished*

The A40 Trunk Road (Old Bath Road, Cheltenham) (Prohibition and Restriction of Waiting) Order 1998 No. 200. Enabling power: *Road Traffic Regulation Act 1984, ss. 1 (1), 2 (1) (2), 4 (1) (2)*. Made: 19.01.1998. Coming into force: 02.02.1998. Effect: None. – *Unpublished*

The A40 Trunk Road (Sandford Road, Cheltenham) (Temporary Restriction of Traffic) Order 1998 No. 68. Enabling power: *Road Traffic Regulation Act 1984, s. 14 (1) (a) (5) (a)*. Made: 12.01.1998. Coming into force: 17.01.1998. Effect: None. – *Unpublished*

The A40 Trunk Road (Western Avenue, Ealing and Hammersmith and Fulham) (Temporary Prohibition of Traffic and Speed Restriction) Order 1998 No. 183. Enabling power: *Road Traffic Regulation Act 1984, s. 14(1)(a) (4)(7)*. Made: 21.01.1998. Coming into force: 26.01.1998. Effect: None. – *Unpublished*

The A46 Trunk Road (Grafton to Ashton-under-Hill) (Temporary Restriction and Prohibition of Traffic) Order 1998 No. 153. Enabling power: *Road Traffic Regulation Act 1984, s. 14 (1) (a)*. Made: 26.01.1998. Coming into force: 02.02.1998. Effect: None. – *Unpublished*

The A46 Trunk Road (Lincoln Bypass) (Temporary Restriction and Prohibition of Traffic) Order 1998 No. 151. Enabling power: *Road Traffic Regulation Act 1984, s. 14 (1) (a)*. Made: 26.01.1998. Coming into force: 02.02.1998. Effect: None. – *Unpublished*

The A46 Trunk Road (Ratcliffe on the Wreake to Six Hills, Leicestershire) (Temporary 40 Miles Per Hour Speed Restriction) Order 1998 No. 101. Enabling power: *Road Traffic Regulation Act 1984, s. 14(1)(a)*. Made: 19.01.1998. Coming into force: 26.01.1998. Effect: None. – *Unpublished*

The A46 Trunk Road (Slip Roads, Leicestershire) (Temporary Prohibition of Traffic) Order 1998 No. 100. Enabling power: *Road Traffic Regulation Act 1984, s. 14 (1) (a)*. Made: 19.01.1998. Coming into force: 26.01.1998. Effect: None. – *Unpublished*

The A46 Trunk Road (Swainswick Support Works) (Temporary Prohibition of Traffic and 30 mph Speed Restriction) Order 1997 Variation Order 1998 No. 87. Enabling power: *Road Traffic Regulation Act 1984, s. 14 (1) (a), sch. 9, para. 27 (1)*. Made: 19.01.1998. Coming into force: 24.01.1998. Effect: S.I. 1997/2794 amended. – *Unpublished*

The A47 Trunk Road (Church Road Junction, Great Plumstead, Norfolk) (Temporary Restriction and Prohibition of Traffic) Order 1998 No. 48. Enabling power: *Road Traffic Regulation Act 1984, s. 14 (1) (a)*. Made: 12.01.1998. Coming into force: 19.01.1998. Effect: None. – *Unpublished*

The A47 Trunk Road (East Dereham Bypass, Norfolk) (Temporary 10 Miles Per Hour and 40 Miles Per Hour Speed Restriction) Order 1998 No. 99. Enabling power: *Road Traffic Regulation Act 1984, s. 14 (1) (a)*. Made: 20.01.1998. Coming into force: 26.01.1998. Effect: None. – *Unpublished*

The A47 Trunk Road (Soke Parkway, Peterborough) (Temporary 30 Miles Per Hour Speed Restriction) Order 1998 No. 97. Enabling power: *Road Traffic Regulation Act 1984, s. 14(1)(a)*. Made: 19.01.1998. Coming into force: 26.01.1998. Effect: None. – *Unpublished*

The A49 Trunk Road (Portway, Hereford & Worcester) (Temporary Restriction and Prohibition of Traffic) Order 1998 No. 147. Enabling power: *Road Traffic Regulation Act 1984, s. 14(1)(a)*. Made: 26.01.1998. Coming into force: 02.02.1998. Effect: None. – *Unpublished*

The A52 Trunk Road (Radcliffe-on-Trent, Nottinghamshire) (Temporary Restriction of Traffic) Order 1998 No. 95. Enabling power: *Road Traffic Regulation Act 1984, s. 14 (1) (a)*. Made: 19.01.1998. Coming into force: 26.01.1998. Effect: None. – *Unpublished*

The A57 Trunk Road (Aston By-Pass) (Temporary Restriction and Prohibition of Traffic) Order 1998 No. 37. Enabling power: *Road Traffic Regulation Act 1984, s. 14 (1) (a)*. Made: 08.01.1998. Coming into force: 15.01.1998. Effect: None. – *Unpublished*

The A58 Trunk Road (Chain Bar - Westfield Lane) (Temporary 40 Miles Per Hour Speed Restriction) Order 1998 No. 89. Enabling power: *Road Traffic Regulation Act 1984, s. 14(1)(a)*. Made: 15.01.1998. Coming into force: 18.01.1998. Effect: None. – *Unpublished*

The A63 and A1041 Trunk Roads (Selby) (Temporary Prohibition of Traffic) Order 1998 No.69. Enabling power: *Road Traffic Regulation Act 1984, s. 14 (1) (a)*. Made: 14.01.1998. Coming into force: 17.01.1998. Effect: None. – *Unpublished*

The A63 Trunk Road (Hemingbrough) (Temporary 10 Miles Per Hour Speed Restriction) Order 1998 No. 199. Enabling power: *Road Traffic Regulation Act 1984, s. 14 (1) (a)*. Made: 28.01.1998. Coming into force: 31.01.1998. Effect: None. – *Unpublished*

The A66 Trunk Road (Kemplay Roundabout to Skirsgill Roundabout) (Temporary 10 Miles Per Hour and 50 Miles Per Hour Speed Restriction) Order 1998 No. 36. Enabling power: *Road Traffic Regulation Act 1984, s. 14 (1) (a)*. Made: 09.01.1998. Coming into force: 10.01.1998. Effect: None. – *Unpublished*

The A78 Trunk Road (High Street and Inverkip Street, Greenock) (Temporary Prohibition of Traffic and Temporary Prohibition of Specified Turns) Order 1998 No. 31. Enabling power: *Road Traffic Regulation Act 1984, s. 14 (1) (a)*. Made: 09.01.1998. Coming into force: 18.01.1998. Effect: None. – *Unpublished*

The A78 Trunk Road (Inverkip Road, Greenock) (Temporary Prohibition of Specified Turns) Order 1998 No. 32. Enabling power: *Road Traffic Regulation Act 1984, s. 14 (1) (a)*. Made: 12.01.1998. Coming into force: 18.01.1998. Effect: None. – *Unpublished*

The A82 Trunk Road (Strowanswell Road Junction, Dumbarton) (Temporary Prohibition of Specified Turns) Order 1998 No. 7. Enabling power: *Road Traffic Regulation Act 1984, s. 14 (1) (a)*. Made: 06.01.1998. Coming into force: 18.01.1998. Effect: None. – *Unpublished*

The A167 Trunk Road (Blind Lane Interchange - Picktree Lane Roundabout) (Temporary Prohibition of Traffic) Order 1998 No. 133. Enabling power: *Road Traffic Regulation Act 1984, s. 14 (1) (a)*. Made: 22.01.1998. Coming into force: 24.01.1998. Effect: None. – *Unpublished*

The A339 Trunk Road (Headley and Kingsclere) (Temporary Speed Restrictions) Order 1998 No. 2. Enabling power: *Road Traffic Regulation Act 1984, s. 14 (1) (a)*. Made: 05.01.1998. Coming into force: 10.01.1998. Effect: None. – *Unpublished*

The A414 Trunk Road (London Colney Roundabout) (Temporary Restriction and Prohibition of Traffic) Order 1998 No. 185. Enabling power: *Road Traffic Regulation Act 1984, s. 14 (1) (a) (5) (b) (7)*. Made: 23.01.1998. Coming into force: 28.01.1998. Effect: None. – *Unpublished*

The A421 and A428 Trunk Roads (Bedfordshire) (Temporary Restriction and Prohibition of Traffic) Order 1998 No. 150. Enabling power: *Road Traffic Regulation Act 1984, s. 14 (1) (a)*. Made: 26.01.1998. Coming into force: 02.02.1998. Effect: None. – *Unpublished*

The A465 Trunk Road (Merthyr Tydfil, Merthyr Tydfil County Borough) (Prescribed Route and Prohibition of Right Hand Turn) Order 1998 No. 28. Enabling power: *Road Traffic Regulation Act 1984, ss. 1 (1), 2 (1) (2)*. Made: 06.01.1998. Coming into force: 19.01.1998. Effect: None. – *Unpublished*

The A483 Trunk Road (Ruabon, Wrexham) (Temporary Prohibition of Vehicles) Order 1998 No.113. Enabling power: *Road Traffic Regulation Act 1984, s. 14 (1) (4)*. Made: 16.01.1998. Coming into force: 19.01.1998. Effect: None. – *Unpublished*

The A523 Trunk Road (Ashbourne Road, Staffordshire) (Temporary 10 Miles Per Hour and 30 Miles Per Hour Speed Restriction) Order 1998 No. 102. Enabling power: *Road Traffic Regulation Act 1984, s. 14 (1) (a)*. Made: 19.01.1998. Coming into force: 26.01.1998. Effect: None. – *Unpublished*

The A580 Trunk Road (East Lancashire Road, Golborne) (Temporary 40 Miles Per Hour Speed Limit) Order 1998 No. 33. Enabling power: *Road Traffic Regulation Act 1984, s. 14 (1)*. Made: 08.01.1998. Coming into force: 11.01.1998. Effect: None. – *Unpublished*

The A596 Trunk Road (Workington Bridge) (Temporary 10 Miles Per Hour Speed Restriction) Order 1998 No. 50. Enabling power: *Road Traffic Regulation Act 1984, s. 14 (1) (a)*. Made: 08.01.1998. Coming into force: 10.01.1998. Effect: None. – *Unpublished*

The A627(M) Motorway (Temporary Prohibition of Traffic) Order 1998 No. 195. Enabling power: *Road Traffic Regulation Act 1984, s. 14 (1)*. Made: 27.01.1998. Coming into force: 30.01.1998. Effect: None. – *Unpublished*

The A627(M) Motorway (Temporary Restriction of Traffic) Order 1998 No. 198. Enabling power: *Road Traffic Regulation Act 1984, s. 14 (1) (a) (7)*. Made: 27.01.1998. Coming into force: 29.01.1998. Effect: None. – *Unpublished*

The A638 Trunk Road (Bawtry Road, Doncaster) (One Way Traffic) Order 1998 No. 52. Enabling power: *Road Traffic Regulation Act 1984, ss. 1 (1), 2 (1) (2)*. Made: 15.01.1998. Coming into force: 19.01.1998. Effect: None. – *Unpublished*

The A725/A726 Trunk Road (High Blantyre) (Temporary Prohibition of Traffic) Order 1998 No.187. Enabling power: *Road Traffic Regulation Act 1984, s. 14 (1) (a)*. Made: 28.01.1998. Coming into force: 09.02.1998. Effect: None. – *Unpublished*

The A6120 Leeds Outer Ring Road (Station Road, Cross Gates) (Temporary Restriction and Prohibition of Traffic) Order 1998 No. 132. Enabling power: *Road Traffic Regulation Act 1984, s. 14 (1) (a)*. Made: 22.01.1998. Coming into force: 25.01.1998. Effect: None. – *Unpublished*

The A6120 Trunk Road (Moor Allerton) (Temporary 30 Miles Per Hour Speed Restriction) Order 1998 No. 9. Enabling power: *Road Traffic Regulation Act 1984, s. 14 (1) (a)*. Made: 02.01.1998. Coming into force: 04.01.1998. Effect: None. – *Unpublished*

The London North Circular Trunk Road (A406) (Pinkham Way, Barnet) (Temporary Prohibition of Traffic) Order 1998 No. 138. Enabling power: *Road Traffic Regulation Act 1984, s. 14 (1) (4)*. Made: 20.01.1998. Coming into force: 26.01.1998. Effect: None. – *Unpublished*

Prices/availability are liable to change without notice

192 *ROAD TRAFFIC: TRAFFIC REGULATION*

The M1 and M69 Motorways (Connecting Roads, Leicestershire) (Temporary Prohibition of Traffic) Order 1998 No. 239. Enabling power: *Road Traffic Regulation Act 1984, s. 14 (1) (a)*. Made: 02.02.1998. Coming into force: 09.02.1998. Effect: None. – *Unpublished*

The M1 Motorway (Junction 35A, Northbound Exit Slip Road) (Temporary Prohibition of Traffic) Order 1998 No. 136. Enabling power: *Road Traffic Regulation Act 1984, s. 14 (1) (a)*. Made: 21.01.1998. Coming into force: 23.01.1998. Effect: None. – *Unpublished*

The M1 Motorway (Junction 46) (Temporary Prohibition of Traffic) Order 1998 No. 247. Enabling power: *Road Traffic Regulation Act 1984, s. 14 (1) (a)*. Made: 05.02.1998. Coming into force: 08.02.1998. Effect: None. – *Unpublished*

The M1 Motorway (Junctions 6 and 8, Slip Roads) (Temporary Prohibition of Traffic) Order 1998 No. 184. Enabling power: *Road Traffic Regulation Act 1984, s. 14 (1) (a)*. Made: 26.01.1998. Coming into force: 31.01.1998. Effect: None. – *Unpublished*

The M1 Motorway (Junctions 33 - 34) (Temporary Restriction of Traffic) Order 1998 No.17. Enabling power: *Road Traffic Regulation Act 1984, s. 14 (1) (a) (7)*. Made: 02.01.1998. Coming into force: 06.01.1998. Effect: None. – *Unpublished*

The M4 Motorway (Brynglas Tunnels, Newport) (Temporary Prohibition of Vehicles and 50 mph Speed Limit) Order 1998 No. 75. Enabling power: *Road Traffic Regulation Act 1984, s. 14 (1) (4) (7)*. Made: 07.01.1998. Coming into force: 09.01.1998. Effect: None. – *Unpublished*

The M4 Motorway (Junctions 6 - 8/9) (Temporary Restriction and Prohibition of Traffic) Order 1998 No. 67. Enabling power: *Road Traffic Regulation Act 1984, s. 14 (1) (a) (7)*. Made: 12.01.1998. Coming into force: 15.01.1998. Effect: None. – *Unpublished*

The M4 Motorway (Junctions 16-18) (Temporary 50 Miles Per Hour Speed Restriction) Order 1998 No. 152. Enabling power: *Road Traffic Regulation Act 1984, s. 14 (1) (a) (7), sch. 9, para. 27 (1)*. Made: 26.01.1998. Coming into force: 31.01.1998. Effect: S.I. 1997/3086 revoked. – *Unpublished*

The M4 Motorway (Junctions 24-28, Coldra-Tredegar Park, Newport) (Temporary Prohibition of Vehicles) Order 1998 No. 368. Enabling power: *Road Traffic Regulation Act 1984, s. 14 (1) (4)*. Made: 20.02.1998. Coming into force: 22.02.1998. Effect: None. – *Unpublished*

The M4 Motorway (Marker Posts 64.8 - 59.2) (Temporary Restriction of Traffic) Order 1998 No.143. Enabling power: *Road Traffic Regulation Act 1984, s. 14 (1) (a) (7)*. Made: 26.01.1998. Coming into force: 31.01.1998. Effect: None. – *Unpublished*

The M5 Motorway (Junction 4) and A38 Trunk Road (Hereford & Worcester) (Temporary 10 Miles Per Hour and 40 Miles Per Hour Speed Restriction) Order 1998 No. 42. Enabling power: *Road Traffic Regulation Act 1984, s. 14 (1) (a)*. Made: 09.01.1998. Coming into force: 16.01.1998. Effect: None. – *Unpublished*

The M5 Motorway (Junctions 14 to 15) (Temporary Prohibition and Restriction of Traffic) Order 1998 No. 38. Enabling power: *Road Traffic Regulation Act 1984, s. 14 (1) (a) (7)*. Made: 05.01.1998. Coming into force: 10.01.1998. Effect: None. – *Unpublished*

The M6 Motorway (Junction 11) (Slip Roads) (Temporary Prohibition of Traffic) Order 1998 No.230. Enabling power: *Road Traffic Regulation Act 1984, s. 14 (1) (a)*. Made: 02.02.1998. Coming into force: 09.02.1998. Effect: None. – *Unpublished*

The M6 Motorway (Junction 27 and 28) (Temporary 50 Miles Per Hour Speed Limit) Order 1998 No.304. Enabling power: *Road Traffic Regulation Act 1984, s. 14 (1) (a) (7)*. Made: 06.02.1998. Coming into force: 08.02.1998. Effect: None. – *Unpublished*

The M6 Motorway (Junction 28, Southbound Exit Slip Road) (Temporary Prohibition of Traffic) Order 1998 No. 65. Enabling power: *Road Traffic Regulation Act 1984, s. 14 (1) (a)*. Made: 14.01.1998. Coming into force: 16.01.1998. Effect: None. – *Unpublished*

The M6 Motorway (Junction 34 and Slip Roads) (Temporary Prohibition and Restriction of Traffic) Order 1998 No. 344. Enabling power: *Road Traffic Regulation Act 1984, s. 14 (1) (a) (7)*. Made: 12.02.1998. Coming into force: 19.02.1998. Effect: None. – *Unpublished*

The M6 Motorway (Junctions 15 - 14) (Temporary Restriction of Traffic) Order 1998 No.233. Enabling power: *Road Traffic Regulation Act 1984, s. 14 (1) (a)*. Made: 02.02.1998. Coming into force: 09.02.1998. Effect: None. – *Unpublished*

The M6 Motorway (Junctions 32 to 33) (Temporary 50 Miles Per Hour Speed Limit) Order 1998 No.41. Enabling power: *Road Traffic Regulation Act 1984, s. 14 (1) (a)*. Made: 08.01.1998. Coming into force: 11.01.1998. Effect: None. – *Unpublished*

The M6 Motorway (Sandwell, West Midlands) (50 Miles Per Hour Speed Limit and Suspension of Regulation 9 of the Motorways Traffic Regulations) (Experimental) Order 1998 No. 94. Enabling power: *Road Traffic Regulation Act 1984, ss. 9(1) to (3), 10(1)(2)*. Made: 19.01.1998. Coming into force: 02.02.1998. Effect: None. – *Unpublished*

The M11 and M25 Motorways (Junction 6 - Northbound M11 to Westbound M25 Link Road) (Temporary Prohibition of Traffic) Order 1998 No. 236. Enabling power: *Road Traffic Regulation Act 1984, s. 14 (1) (a)*. Made: 02.02.1998. Coming into forrce: 07.02.1998. Effect: None. – *Unpublished*

Prices/availability are liable to change without notice

The M11 Motorway (Junction 4 - Northbound Entry Slip Road) (Temporary Prohibition of Traffic) Order 1998 No. 35. Enabling power: *Road Traffic Regulation Act 1984, s. 14 (1) (a).* Made: 09.01.1998. Coming into force: 14.01.1998. Effect: None. – *Unpublished*

The M11 Motorway (Junctions 4 - 6) (Temporary Prohibition of Traffic) Order 1998 No.103. Enabling power: *Road Traffic Regulation Act 1984, s. 14 (1) (a).* Made: 19.01.1998. Coming into force: 24.01.1998. Effect: None. – *Unpublished*

The M11 Motorway (Marker Posts 22.9 - 30.6) (Temporary Restriction and Prohibition of Traffic) Order 1998 No. 379. Enabling power: *Road Traffic Regulation Act 1984, s. 14 (1) (a) (7).* Made: 16.02.1998. Coming into force: 21.02.1998. Effect: None. – *Unpublished*

The M18 Motorway (Wadworth) (Temporary Restriction of Traffic) Order 1998 No. 248. Enabling power: *Road Traffic Regulation Act 1984, s. 14 (1) (a) (7).* Made: 05.02.1998. Coming into force: 08.02.1998. Effect: None. – *Unpublished*

The M20 Motorway (Marker Posts 99.10 - 109.60) (Temporary Restriction of Traffic) Order 1998 No. 297. Enabling power: *Road Traffic Regulation Act 1984, s. 14 (1) (a) (7).* Made: 09.02.1998. Coming into force: 14.02.1998. Effect: None. – *Unpublished*

The M23 Motorway (Marker Posts 30.0 - 37.3) (Temporary Restriction and Prohibition of Traffic) Order 1998 No. 90. Enabling power: *Road Traffic Regulation Act 1984, s. 14 (1) (a) (7).* Made: 19.01.1998. Coming into force: 24.01.1998. Effect: None. – *Unpublished*

The M23 Motorway (Marker Posts 30.0 - 37.3) (Temporary Restriction and Prohibition of Traffic) Order 1998 Variation Order 1998 No. 299. Enabling power: *Road Traffic Regulation Act 1984, s. 14 (1) (a) (7), sch. 9, para. 27 (1).* Made: 09.02.1998. Coming into force: 16.02.1998. Effect: S.I. 1998/90 amended. – *Unpublished*

The M25 Motorway (Junction 18) (Temporary Prohibition of Traffic) Order 1998 No. 298. Enabling power: *Road Traffic Regulation Act 1984, s. 14 (1) (a).* Made: 09.02.1998. Coming into force: 14.02.1998. Effect: None. – *Unpublished*

The M25 Motorway (Junction 19 - 18 Westbound) (Temporary Restriction and Prohibition of Traffic) Order 1998 No. 53. Enabling power: *Road Traffic Regulation Act 1984, s. 14 (1) (a) (7).* Made: 12.01.1998. Coming into force: 17.01.1998. Effect: None. – *Unpublished*

The M25 Motorway (Junction 19 - Eastbound Link Road) (Temporary Prohibition of Traffic) Order 1998 No. 279. Enabling power: *Road Traffic Regulation Act 1984, s. 14 (1) (a).* Made: 30.01.1998. Coming into force: 01.02.1998. Effect: None. *Unpublished*

The M25 Motorway Junction 29 (Temporary 50 Miles Per Hour Speed Restriction) Order 1998 No.134. Enabling power: *Road Traffic Regulation Act 1984, s. 14 (1) (a).* Made: 19.01.1998. Coming into force: 24.01.1998. Effect: None. – *Unpublished*

The M25 Motorway (Marker Posts 132.70 - 139.60) (Temporary Restriction and Prohibition of Traffic) Order 1998 No. 186. Enabling power: *Road Traffic Regulation Act 1984, s. 14 (1) (a) (7).* Made: 26.01.1998. Coming into force: 31.01.1998. Effect: None. – *Unpublished*

The M50 Ross Spur Motorway (Hereford and Worcester) (Temporary Restriction of Traffic) Order 1998 No. 43. Enabling power: *Road Traffic Regulation Act 1984, s. 14 (1) (a) (7).* Made: 09.01.1998. Coming into force: 16.01.1998. Effect: None. – *Unpublished*

The M53 Motorway (Junction 11, Birkenhead to Manchester Link Road) (Temporary Prohibition of Traffic) Order 1998 No. 242. Enabling power: *Road Traffic Regulation Act 1984, s. 14 (1) (a).* Made: 03.02.1998. Coming into force: 10.02.1998. Effect: None. – *Unpublished*

The M56 Motorway (Junction 9, Chester to Birmingham Link Road) (Temporary Prohibition of Traffic) Order 1998 No. 245. Enabling power: *Road Traffic Regulation Act 1984, s. 14 (1) (a).* Made: 05.02.1998. Coming into force: 11.02.1998. Effect: None. – *Unpublished*

The M56 Motorway (Junction 15, the Manchester to Chester Link Road) (Temporary Restriction of Traffic) Order 1998 No. 246. Enabling power: *Road Traffic Regulation Act 1984, s. 14 (1) (a) (7).* Made: 05.02.1998. Coming into force: 09.02.1998. Effect: None. – *Unpublished*

The M58 Motorway (Junction 5, Slip Roads) (Temporary Prohibition of Traffic) Order 1998 No.88. Enabling power: *Road Traffic Regulation Act 1984, s. 14 (1) (a).* Made: 14.01.1998. Coming into force: 18.01.1998. Effect: None. – *Unpublished*

The M61 Motorway and A666 Kearsley Spur, (Southbound Carriageway) (Temporary Restriction of Traffic) Order 1998 No. 249. Enabling power: *Road Traffic Regulation Act 1984, s. 14 (1) (a) (7).* Made: 30.01.1998. Coming into force: 03.02.1998. Effect: None. – *Unpublished*

The M61 Motorway (Bridgeworks) (Temporary Restriction of Traffic) Order 1998 No. 305. Enabling power: *Road Traffic Regulation Act 1984, s. 14 (1) (a) (7).* Made: 06.02.1998. Coming into force: 08.02.1998. Effect: None. – *Unpublished*

The M61 Motorway (Sandhole Loop Bridge) (Temporary Restriction of Traffic) Order 1998 No.182. Enabling power: *Road Traffic Regulation Act 1984, s. 14 (1) (a) (7).* Made: 20.01.1998. Coming into force: 22.01.1998. Effect: None. – *Unpublished*

194 *SOCIAL SECURITY*

The M62 (Junction 18) and the M66 (Junction 4) Motorways (Simister Roundabout) (Temporary Restriction of Traffic) Order 1998 No. 350. Enabling power: *Road Traffic Regulation Act 1984, s. 14 (1) (a) (7).* Made: 13.02.1998. Coming into force: 17.02.1998. Effect: None. – *Unpublished*

The M62 Motorway (Junction 9, Westbound Entry Slip Road) (Temporary Prohibition of Traffic) Order 1998 No. 346. Enabling power: *Road Traffic Regulation Act 1984, s. 14 (1) (a).* Made: 09.02.1998. Coming into force: 12.02.1998. Effect: None. – *Unpublished*

The M62 Motorway (Junction 13, Eastbound Entry Slip Road) (Temporary Prohibition of Traffic) Order 1998 No. 196. Enabling power: *Road Traffic Regulation Act 1984, s. 14 (1) (a).* Made: 27.01.1998. Coming into force: 29.01.1998. Effect: None. – *Unpublished*

The M62 Motorway (Junctions 32-33) (Temporary Restriction and Prohibition of Traffic) Order 1998 No. 51. Enabling power: *Road Traffic Regulation Act 1984, s. 14(1)(a)(7).* Made: 12.01.1998. Coming into force: 14.01.1998. Effect: None. – *Unpublished*

The M62 Motorway (Junctions 35-36) (Temporary Restriction and Prohibition of Traffic) Order 1998 No. 380. Enabling power: *Road Traffic Regulation Act 1984, s. 14(1)(a)(7).* Made: 12.02.1998. Coming into force: 15.02.1998. Effect: None. – *Unpublished*

The M63 Motorway (Junction 3, Northbound Access Slip Road) (Temporary Prohibition of Traffic) Order 1998 No. 66. Enabling power: *Road Traffic Regulation Act 1984, s. 14 (1) (a).* Made: 14.01.1998. Coming into force: 16.01.1998. Effect: None. – *Unpublished*

The M63 Motorway (Junction 3, Southbound Exit Slip Road) (Temporary Prohibition of Traffic) Order 1998 No. 64. Enabling power: *Road Traffic Regulation Act 1984, s. 14 (1) (a).* Made: 13.01.1998. Coming into force: 15.01.1998. Effect: None. – *Unpublished*

The M63 Motorway (Junction 3, Southbound Exit Slip Road) (Temporary Prohibition of Traffic) Order 1998 No. 197. Enabling power: *Road Traffic Regulation Act 1984, s. 14 (1) (a).* Made: 27.01.1998. Coming into force: 29.01.1998. Effect: None. – *Unpublished*

The M66 and M62 Motorways (Slip Roads) (Temporary Prohibition of Traffic) Order 1998 No.348. Enabling power: *Road Traffic Regulation Act 1984, s. 14 (1) (a).* Made: 13.02.1998. Coming into force: 16.02.1998. Effect: None. – *Unpublished*

The M66 Motorway (Junctions 1, 3 and 4 Slip Roads) (Temporary Prohibition of Traffic) Order 1998 No. 345. Enabling power: *Road Traffic Regulation Act 1984, s. 14 (1) (a).* Made: 12.02.1998. Coming into force: 15.02.1998. Effect: None. – *Unpublished*

The M67 Motorway (Junction 3, Eastbound Exit Slip Road) (Temporary Prohibition of Traffic) Order 1998 No. 243. Enabling power: *Road Traffic Regulation Act 1984, s. 14 (1) (a).* Made: 30.01.1998. Coming into force: 01.02.1998. Effect: None. – *Unpublished*

The M180 Motorway (Junctions 3 - 4) (Temporary Restriction of Traffic) Order 1998 No.373. Enabling power: *Road Traffic Regulation Act 1984, s. 14(1)(a)(7).* Made: 13.02.1998. Coming into force: 15.02.1998. Effect: None. – *Unpublished*

The M602 Motorway (Junctions 2 and 3) (Temporary Prohibition of Traffic) Order 1998 No.244. Enabling power: *Road Traffic Regulation Act 1984, s. 14 (1) (a).* Made: 30.01.1998. Coming into force: 01.02.1998. Effect: None. – *Unpublished*

The M602 Motorway (Junctions 3 to 2) (Temporary Restriction of Traffic) Order 1998 No.219. Enabling power: *Road Traffic Regulation Act 1984, s. 14 (1) (a).* Made: 20.01.1998. Coming into force: 22.01.1998. Effect: None. – *Unpublished*

SEA FISHERIES

The Conservation of Seals (Common Seals) (Shetland Islands Area) Order 1991 Revocation Order 1998 No. 923 (S. 49). Enabling power: *Conservation of Seals Act 1970, s. 3 (1), 14 (2)* Issued: 08.04.1998. Made: 23.03.1998. Laid: 08.04.1998. Coming into force: 29.04.1998. Effect: S.I. 1991/2638 revoked. Territorial extent & classification: S. General. – 2p. – 0 11 055761 1 *£0.65*

SHERIFF COURT, SCOTLAND

Act of Sederunt (Fees of Shorthand Writers in the Sheriff Court) (Amendment) 1998 No.999 (S. 57). Enabling power: *Sheriff Court (Scotland) Act 1907, s. 40* Issued: 24.04.1998. Made: 01.04.1998. Laid: 08.04.1998. Coming into force: 01.05.1998. Effect: S.I. 1992/1878; 1997/1118, 1265 amended. Territorial extent & classification: S. General. – 4p. – 0 11 055769 7 *£1.10*

SOCIAL SECURITY

The Council Tax Benefit (General) Amendment Regulations 1998 No. 911. Enabling power: *Social Security Contributions and Benefits Act 1992, ss. 131 (10), 137 (1), 175 (1) (3) (4)* Issued: 07.04.1998. Made: 30.03.1998. Laid: 30.03.1998. Coming into force: 31.03.1998. Effect: S.I. 1997/1841 amended. Territorial extent & classification: E/W/S. General. –2p. – 0 11 065892 2 *£0.65*

The Social Security (Contributions) Amendment (No. 2) Regulations 1998 No. 680. Correction slip dated April 1998. – *Free*

Prices/availability are liable to change without notice

SOCIAL SERVICES, ENGLAND AND WALES

The Residential Care Homes and the Nursing Homes and Mental Nursing Homes (Amendment) Regulations 1998 No. 902. Enabling power: *Residential Homes Act 1984, ss. 5(1), 8, 23(2)(b), 27, 56(4)* Issued: 07.04.1998. Made: 27.03.1998. Laid: 08.04.1998. Coming into force: 01.05.1998. Effect: S.I. 1984/1345, 1578 amended & S.I. 1990/2164; 1992/2007 revoked. Territorial extent & classification: E/W. General. – 2p. – 0 11 065877 9 £0.65

TELEGRAPHS

The Wireless Telegraphy (Control of Interference from Videosenders) Order 19987 No.722. Enabling power: *Wireless Telegraphy Act 1967, s. 7(2)* Issued: 09.04.1998. Made: 10.03.1998. Laid: 16.03.1998. Coming into force: 20.04.1998. Effect: S.I. 1997/1482 amended. This SI has been made in consequence of a defect in SI 1997/1482 and is being sent free of charge to all known recipients of that SI. ONLY those already possessing the original (ISBN 0110647440) otherwise version including the original (ISBN 0110658906) is required. Territorial extent & classification: E/W/S/NI. General. – 4p. – 0 11 065889 2 £1.10

TERMS AND CONDITIONS OF EMPLOYMENT

The Employment Rights (Increase of Limits) Order 1998 No. 924. Enabling power: *Trade Union and Labour Relations (Consolidation) Act 1992, s. 159(1)(2) & Employment Rights Act 1996, ss. 31(7), 120(2), 124(2), 125(7), 186(2), 208(4), 227(2), 236(5).* Issued: 08.04.1998. Made: 30.03.1998. Coming into force: 01.04.1998. Effect: S.I. 1995/1953 amended. Supersedes draft SI ISBN 0110655443 issued 26.02.1998. Territorial extent & classification: E/W/S. General. – 4p. – 0 11 065882 5 £1.10

The Suspension from Work on Maternity Grounds (Merchant Shipping and Fishing Vessels) Order 1998 No. 587. Enabling power: *Employment Rights Act 1972, s. 66(2)* Issued: 22.04.1998. Made: 09.03.1998. Laid: 10.03.1998. Coming into force: 31.03.1998. Effect: None. Territorial extent & classification: E/W/S. General. – Implements provisions of DIR 92/85/EEC on the safety & health of pregnant workers & workers who have recently given birth & are breastfeeding (OJ no. L348, 28/11/92). – 2p. – 0 11 065928 7 £0.65

TRADE MARKS

The Trade Marks (Amendment) Rules 1998 No. 925. Enabling power: *Trade Marks Act 1994, ss. 34(1), 38(2), 39(3), 41(1), 43(2)(3), 63(2), 67(1), 78, sch. 3, para. 11(2)* Issued: 09.04.1998. Made: 30.03.1998. Laid: 31.03.1998. Coming into force: 27.04.1998. Effect: S.I. 1994/2583 amended. Territorial extent & classification: E/W/S/NI/IoM. General. – 6p. – 0 11 065888 4 £1.55

UNITED NATIONS

The Federal Republic of Yugoslavia (United Nations Sanctions) Order 1998 No. 1065. Enabling power: *United Nations Act 1946, s. 1* Issued: 29.04.1998. Made: 22.04.1998. Laid: 23.04.1998. Coming into force: 24.04.1998. Effect: None. Territorial extent & classification: E/W/S/NI. General. – 12p. – 0 11 065944 9 £2.80

The Federal Republic of Yugoslavia (United Nations Sanctions) (Dependent Territories) Order 1998 No. 1064. Enabling power: *United Nations Act 1946, s. 1* Issued: 29.04.1998. Made: 22.04.1998. Laid: 23.04.1998. Coming into force: 24.04.1998. Effect: None. Territorial extent & classification: General. – 12p. – 0 11 065947 3 £2.80

URBAN DEVELOPMENT

The Urban Development Corporations in England (Dissolution) Order 1998 No. 953. Enabling power: *Local Government, Planning and Land Act 1980, s. 166* Issued: 09.04.1998. Made: 02.04.1998. Coming into force: 03.04.1998. Effect: None. Territorial extent: E. Local. – 2p. – 0 11 065887 6 £0.65

VALUE ADDED TAX

The Value Added Tax (Place of Supply of Services) (Amendment) Order 1998 No. 763. Enabling power: *Value Added Tax Act 1994, ss. 7(11), 8(5).* Issued: 15.04.1998. Made: 17.03.1998. Laid: 17.03.1998. Coming into force: 18.03.1998. Effect: S.I. 1992/3121 amended. Territorial extent & classification: E/W/S/NI. General. – 2p. – 0 11 065901 5 £0.65

The Value Added Tax (Sport, Sports Competitions and Physical Education) Order 1998 No.764. Enabling power: *Value Added Tax Act 1994, ss. 31(2), 96(9).* Issued: 15.04.1998. Made: 17.03.1998. Laid: 17.03.1998. Coming into force: In acc. with art. 1. Effect: 1994 c. 23 amended. Territorial extent & classification: E/W/S/NI. General. – 4p. – 0 11 065900 7 £1.10

The Value Added Tax (Supply of Services) (Amendment) Order 1998 No. 762. Enabling power: *Value Added Tax Act 1994, s. 5(4)* Issued: 29.04.1998. Made: 17.03.1998. Laid: 17.03.98. Coming into force: 18.03.1998. Effect: S.I. 1993/1507 amended. Territorial extent & classification: E/W/S/NI. General. – Supersedes SI of same number but different ISBN 011065787X issued on 25.03.1998. – 4p. – 0 11 065943 0 £1.10

WATER RESOURCES, ENGLAND AND WALES

The Environment Agency (Earl Soham Discharge) Order 1998 No. 194. Enabling power: *Water Resources Act 1991, s. 168(2).* Made: 27.01.1998. Coming into force: 28.01.1998. Effect: None. – *Unpublished*

Prices/availability are liable to change without notice

The Mines (Notice of Abandonment) Regulations 1998 No. 892. Enabling power: *Water Resources Act 1991, ss. 91A, 91B (2) (4) (b) (5) (6)* Issued: 01.04.1998. Made: 18.03.1998. Laid: 01.04.1998. Coming into force: 01.07.1998. Effect: None. Territorial extent & classification: E/W. General. – 4p. – 0 11 065855 8 *£1.10*

NUMERICAL LIST OF STATUTORY INSTRUMENTS

1997/	Local government, England and Wales	95	Road traffic
	Local government, Scotland	96	Road traffic
2763		97	Road traffic
2	Road traffic	98	Road traffic
7	Road traffic	99	Road traffic
9	Road traffic	100	Road traffic
10	Road traffic	101	Road traffic
11	Road traffic	102	Road traffic
13	Road traffic	103	Road traffic
14	Road traffic	113	Road traffic
17	Road traffic	132	Road traffic
18	Highways, England and Wales	133	Road traffic
21	Roads and bridges, Scotland	134	Road traffic
28	Road traffic	135	Road traffic
31	Road traffic	136	Road traffic
32	Road traffic	137	Road traffic
33	Road traffic	138	Road traffic
34	Road traffic	142	Road traffic
35	Road traffic	143	Road traffic
36	Road traffic	144	Road traffic
37	Road traffic	145	Road traffic
38	Road traffic	146	Road traffic
39	Road traffic	147	Road traffic
40	Road traffic	148	Road traffic
41	Road traffic	149	Road traffic
42	Road traffic	150	Road traffic
43	Road traffic	151	Road traffic
48	Road traffic	152	Road traffic
49	Road traffic	153	Road traffic
50	Road traffic	154	Road traffic
51	Road traffic	160	Road traffic
52	Road traffic	181	Road traffic
53	Road traffic	182	Road traffic
64	Road traffic	183	Road traffic
65	Road traffic	184	Road traffic
66	Road traffic	185	Road traffic
67	Road traffic	186	Road traffic
68	Road traffic	187	Road traffic
69	Road traffic	194	Water resources, England and Wales
70	Road traffic	195	Road traffic
74	Road traffic	196	Road traffic
75	Road traffic	197	Road traffic
87	Road traffic	198	Road traffic
88	Road traffic	199	Road traffic
89	Road traffic	200	Road traffic
90	Road traffic	219	Road traffic
91	Road traffic	230	Road traffic
92	Road traffic	233	Road traffic
94	Road traffic	236	Road traffic

238	Road traffic	680	Social security
239	Road traffic	686	
242	Road traffic	(S. 33)	Construction contracts
243	Road traffic	687	
244	Road traffic	(S. 34)	Construction contracts
245	Road traffic	718	
246	Road traffic	(S. 36)	Education, Scotland
247	Road traffic	719	
248	Road traffic	(S. 37)	Education, Scotland
249	Road traffic	722	Telegraphs
279	Road traffic	724	
297	Road traffic	(S. 38)	Legal aid and advice, Scotland
298	Road traffic	725	
299	Road traffic	(S. 39)	Legal aid and advice, Scotland
304	Road traffic	746	Referendum
305	Road traffic	748	Civil aviation
315	Civil aviation	752	
316	Civil aviation	(S. 42)	Criminal law, Scotland
317	Civil aviation	762	Value added tax
318	Civil aviation	763	Value added tax
324	Local government, England and Wales	764	Value added tax
327	Civil aviation	781	
328	Civil aviation	(S. 40)	
339	Roads and bridges, Scotland	(C. 16)	Environmental protection
344	Road traffic	798	Education, England and Wales
345	Road traffic	799	Education, England and Wales
346	Road traffic	804	
348	Road traffic	(S. 41)	National Health Service, Scotland
350	Road traffic	822	National Health Service, England and Wales
365	Roads and bridges, Scotland	866	Road traffic
366		867	Road traffic
(S. 14)	Pensions	871	Animals
368	Road traffic	873	
373	Road traffic	(S. 43)	Housing, Scotland
379	Road traffic	874	
380	Road traffic	(S. 44)	Housing, Scotland
587	Terms and conditions of employment	877	Education, England and Wales
599	Public records	879	
611		(C. 19)	Agriculture
(S. 22)	Police	880	Education, England and Wales
633	Police	883	Road traffic
655	Education, England and Wales	884	Road traffic
657		890	
(S. 27)	National Health Service, Scotland	(S. 45)	Court of Session, Scotland
658		891	
(S. 28)	National Health Service, Scotland	(S. 46)	Police
659		892	Water resources, England and Wales
(S. 29)	National Health Service, Scotland	893	Northern Ireland
660		894	
(S. 30)	National Health Service, Scotland	(C. 20)	
672	Industrial and provident societies	(S. 47)	Construction contracts
673	Friendly societies	895	National Health Service, England and Wales
675	Building societies	896	National Health Service, England and Wales
676	Industrial and provident societies	897	National Health Service, England and Wales
		898	Local government, England and Wales

899	Customs and excise	995	Road traffic
900	Legal aid and advice, England and Wales	996	Consumer credit
901	Road traffic	997	Consumer credit
902	Social services, England and Wales	998	Consumer credit
	Public health, England and Wales	999	
903	Education, England and Wales	(S. 57)	Sheriff Court, Scotland
904	Highways, England and Wales	1001	Environmental protection
911	Social Security	1002	Local government, England and Wales
922			Police
(S. 48)	National Health Service, Scotland	1003	Local government, England and Wales
923			Police
(S. 49)	Sea fisheries	1004	Housing, Northern Ireland
924	Terms and conditions of employment	1007	Antarctica
925	Trade marks	1009	
926		(C. 24)	Local government, England and Wales
(S. 50)	National Health Service, Scotland	1010	Fire services
927	Merchant shipping	1011	Merchant shipping
928	Merchant shipping	1012	Merchant shipping
929	Merchant shipping	1013	Merchant shipping
930		1014	Immigration
(C. 21)	Electricity	1015	Channel Tunnel
935	Legal services	1016	Harbours, docks, piers and ferries
938	Road traffic	1018	Osteopaths
944	Pensions	1019	Osteopaths
945	Pensions	1020	Osteopaths
947		1029	
(S. 51)	Rating and valuation	(S. 58)	Roads and bridges, Scotland
948	Local government, England and Wales	1043	Metropolitan and city police districts
953	Urban development		Cabs
954	Agriculture	1044	Medicines
955	Agriculture	1045	Medicines
956	Northern Ireland	1056	Marine pollution
957	National Health Service, England and Wales	1058	Civil aviation
961	Betting, gaming and lotteries	1059	European Communities
962	Betting, gaming and lotteries	1060	European Communities
967		1061	European Communities
(C. 22)	Road traffic	1062	European Communities
968	Petroleum	1063	European Communities
	Pipe-lines	1064	United Nations
969		1065	United Nations
(S. 52)	Legal aid and advice, Scotland	1067	Merchant shipping
970		1068	Merchant shipping
(S. 53)	Legal aid and advice, Scotland	1077	Legal services
971		1103	Nurses, midwives and health visitors
(S. 54)	Legal aid and advice, Scotland	1104	National Health Service, England and Wales
972		1123	Local government, England and Wales
(S. 55)	Legal aid and advice, Scotland	1126	Northern Ireland
977	National Health Service, England and Wales	1127	Northern Ireland
978	Highways, England and Wales		
979	Road traffic		
980	Harbours, docks, piers and ferries		
993			
(S. 56)	Court of Session, Scotland		
994	Food		

LIST OF SUBSIDIARY NUMBERS

C. Commencement orders (bring an act or part of an act into operation)

L. Instruments relating to fees or procedure in courts in England and Wales

N.I. Certain orders in Council relating to Northern Ireland

S. Instruments that extend only to Scotland

(C.)	(S.I.)
16	781
19	879
20	894
21	930
22	967
24	1009

(S.)	(S.I.)
14	366
22	611
27	657
28	658
29	659
30	660
33	686
34	687
36	718
37	719
38	724
39	725
42	752
40	781
41	804
43	873
44	874
45	890
46	891
47	894
48	922
49	923
50	926
51	947
52	969
53	970
54	971
55	972
56	993
57	999
58	1029

ALPHABETICAL INDEX

This index is cumulative, arranged alphabetically by subject terms. The page references at the foot of the page refer to the pagination of the issues of the monthly lists.

A

Act of Sederunt: Court of Session: Rules	180
Act of Sederunt: Court of Session: Rules: Shorthand writers: Fees	180
Act of Sederunt: Court of Session: Rules: Solicitors & notaries public	2
Act of Sederunt: Sheriff Court: Shorthand writers: Fees	194
Adopted persons: Contact register: Fees	120
Advice & assistance: Assistance by way of representation: Scotland	183
Advice & assistance: Financial conditions: Scotland	183
Advice & assistance: Representation: Scotland	6
Advice & assistance: Scotland	183
Agriculture Act 1986: Commencement	179
Agriculture: Animal products: Import & export	1
Agriculture: Arable area: Payments	51
Agriculture: Beef carcases: Classification	1
Agriculture: Feeding stuffs	51
Agriculture: Fertilisers: Mammalian meat & bone meal	179
Agriculture: Hill livestock: Compensatory allowances	51
Agriculture: Mammalian meat & bone meal: Fertilisers	179
Agriculture: Nitrate sensitive areas	51
Agriculture: Potato marketing scheme: Certification of revocation	1
Air navigation	104
Air navigation: Flying restrictions: Bournemouth	51
Air navigation: Flying restrictions: Chippenham	179
Air navigation: Flying restrictions: Dover	179
Air navigation: Flying restrictions: Exhibition of flying	180
Air navigation: Flying restrictions: Harrogate	1, 2
Air navigation: Flying restrictions: HM The Queen's 50th anniversary celebrations	2
Air navigation: Flying restrictions: Perth	180
Air navigation: Flying restrictions: Portadown	180
Air navigation: Flying restrictions: Remembrance Sunday	2
Air navigation: Flying restrictions: Southall	2
Air navigation: Flying restrictions: Southampton Water	2
Air navigation: Flying restrictions: State visit of the President of Brazil	51
Air navigation: Flying restrictions: Sumburgh	51
Air quality	4
Aircraft operators: Accounts & records	3
Animal by-products	1
Animal health: Animal by-products	1
Animal health: Animal products: Import & export	103
Animal health: Specified animal pathogens	103
Animal products: Import & export	1, 103
Animals: Animal products: Import & export	103
Animals: Health: Cattle identification	179
Animals: Mink: Keeping	1
Animals: Specified pathogens	103
Animals: Specified risk material	51
Antarctic	179
Antarctic Act 1994: Commencement	1
Antarctic: Guernsey	1
Antarctic: Isle of Man	1

Pages 1-23 Jan, 51-69 Feb, 103-131 Mar, 179-196 April

Antarctic: Jersey 1
Antarctica: Antarctic Act 1994: Commencement 1
Appropriation: Northern Ireland 117
Arable area: Payments 51
Architects: Housing Grants, Construction & Regenration Act 1996: Commencement orders 103, 104, 108
Area tourist boards: Amending scheme: Scotland 110
Arfon, Flintshire & Rhuddlan: Petty sessional divisions 6
Armenia: Partnership & co-operation agreement: Definition of treaties: European Communities 181
Arms & ammunition: Firearms (Amendment) (No. 2) Act 1997: Commencement 1
Arms decommissioning: Northern Ireland Arms Decommissioning Act 1997: Amnesty period 186
Ashford & St. Peter's Hospitals: National Health Service Trust 111
Ashford Hospital: National Health Service Trust 112
Atlantic Telecommunications Ltd.: Public telecommunication systems 129
Aviation: Civil Aviation Act 1982: Jersey 180
AXS Telecom (UK) Ltd.: Public telecommunication systems 67
Azerbaijan: Partnership & co-operation agreement: Definition of treaties: European Communities 182

B

Basildon District Council: Local government: Defined activities: Exemption 110
Bay Community: National Health Service Trust 111
Beef bones 4
Beef carcases: Classification 1
Beef: Labelling: Enforcement 107
Berkshire County Council: Local government: Staff transfer 109
Berkshire: Coroners 104
Betting, gaming & lotteries: Gaming (Bingo) Act: Fees 103
Betting, gaming & lotteries: Gaming Act 1968: Fees: Variation 103
Betting, gaming & lotteries: Gaming Act: Monetary limits: Variation 179
Betting, gaming & lotteries: Gaming Board: Fees 103
Betting, gaming & lotteries: Gaming clubs: Hours & charges 179
Birmingham northern relief road & connecting roads 55
Birmingham northern relief road: Toll 55
Births, deaths, marriages, etc.: Registration: Fees: Scotland 110, 120
Bishop Auckland Hospitals: National Health Service Trust 111
Bone meal: Fertilisers 179
Bread & flour 54
Broadcasting Act 1996: Commencement 51
Broadcasting: Channel 4: Excess revenues: Application of 1
Broadcasting: Digital terrestrial sound: Technical service 103
Broadcasting: National radio mulitplex revenue: Percentage 51
Brunei: Appeals 56
Building societies: Accounts & related provisions 103
Building societies: Charges & fees 179
Building societies: Transfer of business 103

C

Cabs: London cabs 179, 185
Cambridgeshire County Council: City of Peterborough: Local government: Staff transfer 109
Canada: Social security: Contributions & industrial injuries 67
Canadian navigation service: Civil aviation 52
Canterbury & Thanet Community Healthcare: National Health Service Trust 111
Capital gains tax: Annual exempt amount 129
Carriage by air: Acts: Application of provisions 180
Cars: Value added tax 130
Cattle identification 179
Channel 4: Excess revenues: Application of 1
Channel Tunnel: Carriers' liability 179

Pages 1-23 Jan, 51-69 Feb, 103-131 Mar, 179-196 April

Charter trustees: Hereford 109
Cheshire County Council: Borough of Halton & Warrington: Local government: Staff transfer 109
Cheshire: Coroners 52
Chester Waterworks Company: Constitution & regulation 68
Cheviot & Wansbeck, North Tyneside Health Care: National Health Service Trust 112
Chichester Priority Care Services: National Health Service Trust 57
Child abduction & custody: Parties to conventions 51
Child support: Family law 4, 21
Children & young persons: Child abduction & custody: Parties to conventions 51
Children & young persons: National Health Service: Pilot schemes 103, 114, 117, 127, 130
Children & young persons: Protection at work 51
Church of England: Church representation: Rules 54
Church representation: Rules 54
Civil aviation 104
Civil Aviation Act 1982: Jersey 180
Civil aviation: Canadian navigation service 52
Civil aviation: Carriage by Air Acts: Application of provisions 180
Civil aviation: Flying restrictions 1, 2, 51, 179, 180
Civil aviation: Joint financing 2
Civil aviation: Navigation services charges 104
Civil evidence: Northern Ireland 8
Civil legal aid: Financial conditions: Scotland 183
Civil legal aid: Resources: Assessment 109
Civil legal aid: Scotland 183
Civilians: Personal injuries 58
Clean air: Smoke control areas: Exempted fireplaces 2
Coinage: Pyx: Trial of 52
Common agricultural policy: Wine 103
Community Health Care: North Durham: National Health Service Trust 185
Conservation: Natural habitats 2, 23
Conservation: Seals: Shetland Islands area 194
Construction Board: Industrial training levy 106
Construction contracts: Exclusion: Scotland 180
Construction contracts: Housing Grants, Construction & Regeneration Act 1996: Commencement: Scotland 180
Construction contracts: Scheme: Scotland 180
Construction: Contracts: England & Wales 104
Construction: Contracts: Exclusion order: England & Wales 104
Construction: Housing Grants, Construction & Regeneration Act 1996: Commencement orders . . 103, 104, 108
Consular fees 54
Consumer credit: Monetary amounts: Further increase 180
Consumer credit: Monetary limits: Increase 180
Consumer credit: Pawn: Realisation 180
Consumer protection: Cosmetic products: Safety 2
Consumer protection: Recreational craft 52
Consumer protection: Wheeled child conveyances: Safety 2
Contracting out: Crown lands: Management of: Functions in relation to 52
Controlled waste: Carriers: Registration: Seizure of vehicles 106
Copyright & rights: Databases 2, 9
Copyright: Broadcasts & cable programmes: Educational recording: Licensing scheme 104
Coroners Act 1988: Amendment: Local government: Reorganisation 104
Coroners: Berkshire 104
Coroners: Cheshire 52
Coroners: Devon 52
Coroners: Essex 52
Coroners: Hereford & Worcester 52
Coroners: Kent 52
Coroners: Lancashire 52
Coroners: Nottinghamshire 52
Coroners: Peterborough 52

Pages 1-23 Jan, 51-69 Feb, 103-131 Mar, 179-196 April

Coroners: Shropshire 52
Cosmetic products: Safety 2
Council tax & non-domestic rating: Demand notices: Rural rate relief: England 2, 8
Council tax benefit: General 194
Council tax: Administration & enforcement: England & Wales 52
Council tax: Demand notices: Wales 104
Council tax: Discount disregards: England & Wales 52
Council tax: Discounts: Scotland 104
Council tax: Exempt dwellings & discount disregards: England & Wales 53
Council tax: Exempt dwellings: Scotland 104
Council tax: New parishes 2, 6
Council tax: Prescribed classes of dwellings: Wales 53
Council tax: Reduction scheme: Local government: Wales 104
Council tax: Transitional reduction: Local government: Changes: England 53
Countryside: Conservation: Natural habitats, &c. 2, 23
Court of Session: Rules 180
Court of Session: Rules: Shorthand writers: Fees: Act of Sederunt 180
Court of Session: Rules: Solicitors & notaries public 2
Courts: Court of Session: Rules 180
Cows: Suckler: Premium quotas 1
Craft: Recreational 52
Crawley Horsham: National Health Service Trust 112
Credit unions: Fees 183
Crew accommodation: Fishing vessels 184
Crime & Punishment (Scotland) Act 1997: Commencement 3
Crime: Pre-sentence report: Disclosure: Prosecutors: Prescription 53
Criminal Justice & Public Order Act 1994: Commencement & transitional provision 53
Criminal Justice & Public Order Act 1994: Custody Officer certificate: Suspension 127
Criminal Justice (International Co-operation) Act 1990: Overseas forfeiture orders: Enforcement 3
Criminal Justice (International Co-operation) Act 1990: Overseas forfeiture orders: Enforcement 3
Criminal Justice Act 1988: Designated countries & territories 3
Criminal Justice Act 1991: Notice of transfer 105
Criminal law: Criminal Justice & Public Order Act 1994: Commencement & transitional provision 53
Criminal law: Criminal Justice (International Co-operation) Act 1990: Overseas forfeiture orders: Enforcement 3
Criminal law: Criminal Justice Act 1988: Designated countries & territories 3
Criminal law: Criminal Justice Act 1991: Notice of transfer 105
Criminal law: Criminal Procedure and Investigations Act 1996: Appointed day 105
Criminal law: Drug Trafficking Act 1994: Designated countries & territories 3
Criminal law: Northern Ireland 3, 53
Criminal law: Northern Ireland orders: Enforcement: Scotland 180
Criminal law: Pre-sentence report: Disclosure: Prosecutors: Prescription 53
Criminal law: Scotland 3
Criminal legal aid: Prescribed proceedings: Scotland 6, 183
Criminal Procedure & Investigations Act 1996: Appointed day 3
Criminal Procedure & Investigations Act 1996: Appointed day: Northern Ireland 3
Criminal Procedure & Investigations Act 1996: Code of practice: Northern Ireland 3
Criminal Procedure and Investigations Act 1996: Appointed day 105
Crown lands: Management of: Functions in relation to: Contracting out 52
Customs & excise: Aircraft operators: Accounts & records 3
Customs & excise: Dual-use & related goods: Export control 180
Customs & excise: Excise duty point: External & internal Community transit procedure 53
Customs & excise: Export control: Dual-use & related goods 53
Customs & excise: Revenue traders: Accounts & records 3
Customs & excise: United Nations sanctions: Sierra Leone 3

D

Dangerous drugs: Misuse 105
Dangerous drugs: Misuse of Drugs Act 1971: Modification 105

Pages 1-23 Jan, 51-69 Feb, 103-131 Mar, 179-196 April

Dangerous drugs: Misuse: Designation 105
Dangerous substances: Classification: Surface waters: Scotland 69
Darlington Memorial Hospital: National Health Service Trust 112
Databases: Copyright & rights 2, 9
Deck officers & engineer officers: Fishing vessels 184
Deep Sea Mining (Temporary Provisions) Act 1981: Guernsey 3
Deep Sea Mining (Temporary Provisions) Act 1981: Jersey 3
Defence: Visiting forces & international headquarters: Application of law 53
Dental charges: National Health Service 113
Dental charges: National Health Service: Scotland 117
Dental qualifications: European Communities 105
Dentists: Dental qualifications: European Communities 105
Department of Transport: Fees 107
Derby City General Hospital: National Health Service Trust 112
Derbyshire Royal Infirmary: National Health Service Trust 112
Derbyshire: Southern Derbyshire Acute Hospitals: National Health Service Trust 115
Deregulation: Licence transfers 53
Deregulation: Northern Ireland 8
Derwentside District Council: Local government: Defined activities: Exemption 110
Destructive animals: Mink: Keeping 1
Devon County Council: City of Plymouth & Borough of Torbay: Local government: Staff transfer 109
Devon: Coroners 52
Devon: North & East Devon Health Authority: National Health Service 57
Devon: Youth court panels 69
Diocese of Bath & Wells: Educational endowments 105
Diocese of Ely: Educational endowments 3
Diocese of Guildford: Educational endowments 3
Diocese of Oxford: Educational endowments 105
Diocese of Salisbury: Educational endowments 4
Diocese of Southwark: Educational endowments 54
Diocese of St Albans: Educational endowments 105
Diplomatic service: Consular fees 54
Direct grant schools 4
Disability Discrimination: Disabled Persons (Employment) Act 1944: Repeal section 17 105
Disabled Persons (Employment) Act 1944: S.17 & sch. 2: Repeal 105
Disciplinary practice & procedures: Employment protection: Code of practice 22
Disclosure of information: Employment protection: Code of practice 22
District registries: Land registration 56
Doncaster Royal Infirmary & Montagu Hospital: National Health Service Trust 57
Double taxation: Relief: Falkland Islands 5
Double taxation: Relief: Lesotho 5
Double taxation: Relief: Malaysia 5
Double taxation: Relief: Singapore 5
Driving licences: Motor vehicles 10, 121
Drug Trafficking Act 1994: Designated countries & territories 3
Drugs & appliances: Charges: National Health Service 113
Drugs & appliances: Charges: National Health Service: Scotland 116
Drugs: Misuse 105
Drugs: Misuse of Drugs Act 1971: Modification 105
Drugs: Misuse: Designation 105
Dual-use & related goods: Export control 53, 180
Durham County Priority Services: National Health Service Trust 112
Durham: Community Health Care: North Durham: National Health Service Trust 185
Durham: North Durham Acute Hospitals: National Health Service Trust 114
Durham: North Durham Health Care: National Health Service Trust 115
Durham: South Durham: National Health Service Trust 115
Dwellings: Prescribed classes: Council tax: Wales 53

Pages 1-23 Jan, 51-69 Feb, 103-131 Mar, 179-196 April

E

East London & the City Health Authority: National Health Service Trust	185
East Surrey Healthcare: National Health Service Trust	112
East Surrey Priority Care: National Health Service Trust	112
Easynet Group Plc.: Public telecommunication systems	129
Ecclesiastical law: Church of England: Church representation: Rules	54
Ecclesiastical law: United Reformed Church Acts 1972 & 1981: Jersey	105
ECU contracts: Financial markets & insolvency	54
Education (Student Loans) Act 1998: Commencement	54
Education Act 1997: Commencement & transitional provisions	105
Education: Diocese of Bath & Wells: Educational endowments	105
Education: Diocese of Ely: Educational endowments	3
Education: Diocese of Guildford: Educational endowments	3
Education: Diocese of Oxford: Educational endowments	105
Education: Diocese of Salisbury: Educational endowments	4
Education: Diocese of Southwark: Educational endowments	54
Education: Diocese of St Albans: Educational endowments	105
Education: Direct grant schools	4
Education: Education support & training: Grants: England	4
Education: Employment: Modification of enactments	54
Education: Grant	4
Education: Grant-maintained & grant-maintained special schools	181
Education: Grant-maintained schools: New: Finance	181
Education: Hyde-Clarendon College: Dissolution	54
Education: Individual pupils' achievements: Information	181
Education: Listed bodies	105
Education: Local authority inspections: Reports: Publication	181
Education: Local education authorities: Behaviour support plans	106
Education: Local government: Changes: England	110
Education: London Residuary Body: Property transfer	106
Education: Mandatory awards	54
Education: Nursery: England	106
Education: School teachers: Pay & conditions	181
Education: Special needs: Independent schools: Approval	106
Education: Student loans	54
Education: Student loans: Northern Ireland	58
Education: Support & training: Grants	106
Education: Support & training: Grants: England	105
Education: Teacher training: Funding	54
Education: Teachers' pensions	4
Education: Teachers: Premature retirement & redundancy: Compemsation: Scotland	181
Education: Teachers: Superannuation: Scotland	181
Educational Recording Agency Ltd.: Copyright: Broadcasts & cable programmes: Licensing scheme	104
Electrical equipment: Certification: Explosive atmospheres	55
Electricity: Fossil Fuel Levy Act 1998: Commencement	181
Electromagnetic compatibility: Wireless telegraphy: Apparatus: Certification & examination: Fees	4
Employment & training: Construction Board: Industrial training levy	106
Employment & training: Engineering Construction Board: Industrial training levy	106
Employment protection: Disciplinary practice & procedures: Code of practice	22
Employment protection: Disclosure of information: Code of practice	22
Employment protection: Time off: Code of practice	22
Employment rights: Increase of limits	195
Employment: Education: Modification of enactments	54
Employment: Terms & conditions	195
Employment: Terms & conditions: Merchant shipping & fishing vessels	195
Employment: Terms & conditions: Social security: Benefits: Up-rating	128, 130
Engineering Construction Board: Industrial training levy	106
Enterprise zones: Sunderland & Tyne Riverside	106

Pages 1-23 Jan, 51-69 Feb, 103-131 Mar, 179-196 April

Environment Act 1995: Commencement 4, 106
Environment Act 1995: Commencement: Scotland 181
Environment Agency: Earl Soham discharge 195
Environment protection: Environment Act 1995: Commencement 106
Environment, transport & the regions: Secretary of State 7
Environmental effects: Assessment: Offshore petroleum: Production & pipelines 187
Environmental protection: Air quality 4
Environmental protection: Controlled waste: Carriers: Registration: Seizure of vehicles 106
Environmental protection: Environment Act 1995: Commencement 4
Environmental protection: Financial assistance 107, 181
Environmental protection: Hazardous waste incineration: Prescribed processes 106
Environmental protection: Hexachloroethane: Controls 106
Environmental protection: Highway litter: Clearance & cleaning: Transfer of responsibility 106
Environmental protection: Waste management: Licensing 107
Environmental protection: Waste recycling payments 106
Esprit Telecom UK Ltd.: Public telecommunication systems 129
Essex County Council: Boroughs of Southend-on-Sea & Thurrock: Local government: Staff transfer 109
Essex: Coroners 52
Eurobell (Holdings) Plc.: Public telecommunication systems 67
European Communities: Definition of treaties: Europe agreement: Association: Slovenia 181
European Communities: Definition of treaties: European Police Office 4
European Communities: Definition of treaties: Partnership & co-operation agreement: Armenia 181
European Communities: Definition of treaties: Partnership & co-operation agreement: Azerbaijan 182
European Communities: Definition of treaties: Partnership & co-operation agreement: Georgia 181
European Communities: Definition of treaties: Partnership & co-operation agreement: Uzbekistan 181
European Communities: Dentists: Dental qualifications 105
European Communities: Designation 107
European Communities: European Police Office: Immunities & privileges 4
European Convention on Extradition Order 1990 54
European Economic Area: Immigration 5
European Parliamentary elections: Day of by-election: Yorkshire South constituency 120
European Police Office: Definition of treaties: European Communities 4
European Police Office: Immunities & privileges: European Communities 4
Excise duty point: External & internal Community transit procedure 53
Exempt dwellings: Council tax: Scotland 104
Exmouth Docks Harbour: Revision 182
Explosive atmospheres: Electrical equipment: Certification 55
Export control: Dual-use & related goods 53, 180
Export of goods: United Nations sanctions: Sierra Leone 3
Extradition: European Convention on 54
Eygpt: Potatoes: Originating in 58

F

Falkland Islands: Constitution 22
Falkland Islands: Double taxation relief 5
Family law: Child support 4, 21
Fats: Spreadable: Marketing standards 107
Federal Republic of Yugoslavia: Dependent territories: United Nations sanctions 195
Federal Republic of Yugoslavia: United Nations sanctions 195
Feeding stuffs 51
Fees & charges: Department of Transport 107
Felling: Restrictions: Exceptions: Forestry 107
Fertilisers: Mammalian meat & bone meal 179
Finance Act 1989: Section 178 (1): Appointed day 108, 129
Finance Act 1997: Commencement 121
Finance: Local government: New parishes 2, 6
Financial assistance: Environmental protection 107, 181
Financial markets & insolvency: ECU contracts 54

Pages 1-23 Jan, 51-69 Feb, 103-131 Mar, 179-196 April

Financial provisions: Northern Ireland 117
Financial Services Act 1986: Miscellaneous exemptions 4
Fire protection: Large ships: Merchant shipping 185
Fire protection: Small ships: Merchant shipping 185
Fire services: Superannuation: Firemen: Pension scheme 182
Firearms (Amendment) (No. 2) Act 1997: Commencement 1
Firemen: Pension scheme 182
Fireplaces: Exempted: Smoke control areas 2
Fish: Oil & chemical pollution: Food protection 119
Fishery products & live shellfish: Hygiene: Food safety 182
Fishing vessels: Crew accommodation 184
Fishing vessels: Deck officers & engineer officers 184
Fishing vessels: Life-saving appliances 185
Fishing vessels: Merchant shipping: Health & safety at work 7
Fishing vessels: Safety provisions 185
Fishing: Sea: Community quota measures: Enforcement 127
Fishing: Third country: Enforcement 127
Flintshire: Arfon & Rhuddlan: Petty sessional divisions 6
Flour & bread 54
Food protection: Emergency prohibitions: Sheep: Radioactivity 58, 59
Food protection: Emergency prohibitions: Sheep: Radioactivity: Wales 58, 59
Food protection: Fish: Oil & chemical pollution 119
Food safety: Fishery products & live shellfish: Hygiene 182
Food: Beef bones 4
Food: Beef: Labelling: Enforcement 107
Food: Bread & flour 54
Food: Inspections & controls: Charges 55
Food: Pistachios: From Iran: Emergency control 5
Food: Specified risk material 55
Food: Spreadable fats: Marketing standards 107
Food: Welfare 107
Forestry: Felling: Restrictions: Exceptions 107
Forfeited property: Knives: Northern Ireland 53
Fossil Fuel Levy Act 1998: Commencement 181
Freeman Group of Hospitals: National Health Service Trust 112
Frenchay Healthcare: National Health Service Trust 57
Friendly societies 5
Friendly societies: General charge & fees 182
Frontel Communications Ltd.: Public telecommunication systems 67
Fund-holding practices: National Health Service 113
Furness Hospitals: National Health Service Trust 112

G

Galleries & museums: Northern Ireland 58
Gaming (Bingo) Act 1985: Fees 103
Gaming Act 1968: Fees: Variation 103
Gaming Act: Monetary limits: Variation 179
Gaming Clubs: Hours & charges 179
Gateshead Health: National Health Service Trust 113
Gateshead Healthcare: National Health Service Trust 113
Gateshead Hospitals: National Health Service Trust 113
General medical practice: Vocational training: National Health Service 111, 114, 117
General medical practice: Vocational training: National Health Service: Scotland 7
General medical services: National Health Service 114
General medical services: National Health Service: Scotland 7
General Optical Council: Registration & enrolment: Rules 8
General Osteopathic Council: Conditional registration 186
General Osteopathic Council: Constitution & procedure 186

Pages 1-23 Jan, 51-69 Feb, 103-131 Mar, 179-196 April

General Osteopathic Council: Transitional period: Registration & fees: Application 186
Georgia: Partnership & co-operation agreement: Definition of treaties: European Communities 181
Glamorgan: Mid Glamorgan Ambulance: National Health Service Trust 113
Glan Hafren: National Health Service Trust 113
Glan-y-Môr: National Health Service Trust 113
Goods & services: Local authorities: Public bodies 56, 109
Goods vehicles: Type approval: Great Britain 10
Goods: Export of: United Nations sanctions: Sierra Leone 3
Grant-maintained & grant-maintained special schools 181
Grant-maintained & grant-maintained special schools: Finance: Wales 105
Grant-maintained schools: New: Finance 181
Great Britain: Plant health 8
Greater London Authority: Referendum 187
GT UK Ltd.: Public telecommunication systems 67
Guernsey: Antarctic 1
Guernsey: Deep sea mining 3
Guernsey: Oil pollution & general provisions: Merchant shipping 57
Gwent: Youth court panels 69

H

Hairmyres & Stonehouse Hospitals: National Health Service Trust 185
Hampshire: Youth court panels 69
Harbours, docks, piers & ferries: Exmouth docks 182
Harbours, docks, piers & ferries: Ipswich Port Authority 107
Harbours, docks, piers & ferries: Port of Birkenhead Harbour: Empowerment 182
Harbours, docks, piers & ferries: Porthmadog Harbour revision 107
Harefield Hospital: National Health Service: Trust 112
Haringey: London Borough: Trunk roads: Red route: Bus lanes 188
Harlow District Council: Local government: Defined activities: Exemption 56
Hazardous waste: Incineration: Prescribed processes 106
Health & safety at work: Merchant shipping & fishing vessels 7
Health & safety: Enforcing authority 107
Health & safety: Explosive atmospheres: Electrical equipment: Certification 55
Health & safety: Lead: Control of: Work 107
Health authorities: Functions: Prescribed incentive schemes: National Health Service 113
Health Service: National 57
Health Service: National Trusts 57, 111, 112, 113, 114, 115, 116, 184, 185, 186
Health Service: National: Medical practitioner: Choice 113
Health Service: National: Pilot schemes 103, 114, 117, 127, 130
Health Service: National: Pilot schemes: Practitioners 114, 117
Health Service: National: Service committees & tribunal 114
Health visitors, nurses & midwives: Professional conduct 186
Health: Animals: Cattle identification 179
Health: Plants 118
Health: Plants: Potatoes: Originating in: Egypt 58
Heathlands Mental Health: National Health Service Trust 112
Hereford & Worcester: Coroners 52
Hereford & Worcester: Local government: Staff transfer 109
Hereford: Charter trustees 109
Hertfordshire: Combined probation areas 119
Hertfordshire: North: District council: Local government: Defined activities: Exemption 56
Hexachloroethane: Controls: Environmental protection 106
Highway litter: Clearance & cleaning: Transfer of responsibility 106
HighwayOne Corporation Ltd.: Public telecommunication systems 68
Highways: England & Wales: A45 Nene Valley Way widening 182
Highways: England & Wales: Birmingham northern relief road: Toll 55
Highways: England & Wales: Special roads 55
Highways: England & Wales: Trunk roads 5, 55, 107, 108

Pages 1-23 Jan, 51-69 Feb, 103-131 Mar, 179-196 April

Highways: England & Wales: Tunnels 182
Highways: Street works: Inspection fees 182
Hill livestock: Compensatory allowances 51
Homeless persons: Priority need: Scotland 5
Homelessness & housing accommodation: Immigration control: Persons subject to 56
Horton General Hospital: National Health Service Trust 113
Housing accommodation & homelessness: Immigration control: Persons subject to 56
Housing accommodation & homelessness: Persons subject to immigration control: Northern Ireland 182
Housing benefit: Permitted totals 127
Housing Grants, Construction & Regeneration Act 1996: Commencement orders 103, 104, 108
Housing Grants, Construction & Regeneration Act 1996: Commencement: Scotland 180
Housing Revenue Account General Fund: Contribution limits: Scotland 56
Housing support grant: Scotland 182
Housing: Construction contracts: Exclusion: Scotland 180
Housing: Construction contracts: Scheme: Scotland 180
Housing: Landlord: Change: Disposal cost by instalments: Payment 56
Housing: Priority need: Scotland 5
Housing: Relocation grants: Form of application 108
Housing: Renewal grants: Prescribed form & particulars 108
Housing: Renewal: Grants 108
Housing: Residential property: Management practice: Codes: Approval 5
Housing: Right to buy: Charges: Priority 56
Hyde-Clarendon College: Dissolution 54

I

IDT Global Ltd.: Public telecommunication systems 68
Immigration control: Housing accommodation & homelessness: Persons subject to 56
Immigration control: Persons subject to: Housing accommodation & homelessness: Northern Ireland . . . 182
Immigration: European Economic Area 5
Immigration: Transit visa 5, 182
Import & export: Animal products 103
Incapacity for work: Social security 128
Income tax: Double taxation relief: Falkland Islands 5
Income tax: Double taxation relief: Lesotho 5
Income tax: Double taxation relief: Malaysia 5
Income tax: Double taxation relief: Singapore 5
Income tax: Finance Act 1989: Section 178 (1): Appointed day 108, 129
Income tax: Indexation 129
Income tax: Interest rate 108, 129
Income tax: Retirement benefits schemes: Discretion to approve: Restriction 108
Income tax: Retirement benefits schemes: Earnings cap: Indexation 108
Income-related benefits: Subsidy to authorities 127
Industrial & provident societies: Credit unions: Fees 183
Industrial & provident societies: Fees 183
Industrial injuries: Dependency: Permitted earnings limits: Social security 128
Industry training levy: Construction Board 106
Industry training levy: Engineering Construction Board 106
Inheritance tax: Finance Act 1989: Section 178 (1): Appointed day 108, 129
Inheritance tax: Indexation 108
Inheritance tax: Interest rate 108, 129
Injuries: War: Compensation: Shore employments 108
Injury benefits: National Health Service 114
Inspections & controls: Charges 55
Institute of Legal Executives 183
Insurance companies: Accounts & statements 5
Insurance premium tax 6
Insurance: Compulsory: Trans-shipped fish: Ships receiving: Merchant shipping 57
Insurance: Fees 109

Pages 1-23 Jan, 51-69 Feb, 103-131 Mar, 179-196 April

ALPHABETICAL INDEX

Interest rate: Taxes 108, 129
Interference: Videosenders: Telegraphs 195
International immunities & privileges: OSPAR Commission 6
Internet Network Services Ltd.: Public telecommunication systems 68
Interviews: Silent video recording of: Northern Ireland (Emergency Provisions) Act 1996 58
Ipswich Port Authority: Dissolution 107
Iran: Pistachios from: Emergency control 5
Isle of Man: Antarctic 1
Isle of Wight Healthcare: National Health Service Trust 57
Isle of Wight: Parishes: Local government 183
Izencom Ltd.: Public telecommunication systems 68

J

Jersey: Antarctic 1
Jersey: Civil Aviation Act 1982 180
Jersey: Deep sea mining 3
Jobseeker's allowance 21
Judicial committee: Brunei: Appeals 56
Justices of the Peace: Petty sessional divisions 6

K

KDD Europe Ltd.: Public telecommunication systems 68
Kent County Council: Borough of Gillingham & City of Rochester upon Medway: Local government: Staff
transfer 109
Kent: Coroners 52
Kent: North Kent Healthcare: National Health Service Trust 112
Kent: South Kent Community Healthcare: National Health Service Trust 116
Knives: Forfeited property: Northern Ireland 53

L

Lancashire County Council: Boroughs of Blackburn with Darwen & Blackpool: Local government: Staff transfer 109
Lancashire: Coroners 52
Lancaster Acute Hospitals: National Health Service Trust 113
Lancaster Priority Services: National Health Service Trust 113
Land Registration Act 1997: Commencement 6
Land registration: District registries 56
Land registration: Rules 6
Landfill tax 6
Landlord. Change: Disposal cost by instalments: Payment 56
Lands tribunal: Rules 6
Law Hospital: National Health Service Trust 185
Law: Criminal: Criminal Justice & Public Order Act 1994: Commencement & transitional provision 53
LCI Telecom UK Ltd.: Public telecommunication systems 129
Lead: Control of: Work: Health & safety 107
Lee Valley Regional Park Authority: London Docklands Development Corporation: Property, etc.: Transfer 130
Leeds Community & Mental Health Services Teaching: National Health Service Trust 57
Leeds Teaching Hospitals: National Health Service Trust 113
Leeds: United Leeds Teaching Hospitals: National Health Service Trust 116
Legal advice & assistance 109
Legal aid & advice 109
Legal aid & advice, Scotland: Criminal legal aid: Prescribed proceedings 183
Legal aid & advice: Civil: Resources: Assessment 109
Legal aid & advice: Civil: Scotland 183
Legal aid & advice: Criminal & care proceedings 109
Legal aid & advice: Criminal legal aid: Prescribed proceedings: Scotland 6

Pages 1-23 Jan, 51-69 Feb, 103-131 Mar, 179-196 April

Legal aid & advice: Representation: Scotland 6
Legal aid & advice: Scotland 183
Legal aid: Criminal & care proceedings 109
Legal aid: Mediation: Family matters 183
Legal services ombudsman: Jurisdiction 183
Legal services: Institute of Legal Executives 183
Legal services: Ombudsman: Commissioner for Local Administration: Scotland 57
Leicestershire: Combined probation areas 119
Lesotho: Double taxation relief 5
Lewisham & Guy's Mental Health: National Health Service Trust 185
Licence transfers: Deregulation 53
Licensing: Fees 57
Lifespan Health Care Cambridge: National Health Service Trust 185
Lincoln District Healthcare: National Health Service Trust 57
Lincolnshire Ambulance & Health Transport Service: National Health Service Trust 185
Llandough Hospital & Community: National Health Service Trust 116
Local authorities: Capital finance 56, 110
Local authorities: Capital finance: Rate of discount 1998/99 109
Local authorities: Goods & services: Public bodies 56, 109, 183
Local authorities: Members' allowances 109, 110
Local authorities: Requisite calculations: Alteration 56
Local authorities: Transport charges 183
Local authority inspections: Education: Reports: Publication 181
Local education authorities: Behaviour support plans 106
Local elections: Parishes & communities 120
Local elections: Principal areas 120
Local Government & Rating Act 1997: Commencement 110
Local Government Act 1988: Defined activities: Exemption: Basildon, Derwentside & Salisbury District Councils 110
Local Government Act 1988: Defined activities: Exemption: Maidstone Borough Council 110
Local government Area tourism boards: Amending scheme: Scotland 110
Local government Staff Commission: Winding-up: England 184
Local government: Changes: Rent Act registration areas 6
Local government: Charter trustees: Hereford 109
Local government: Council tax: Reduction scheme: Wales 104
Local government: Council tax: Transitional reduction: Changes: England 53
Local government: Defined activities: Exemption 110
Local government: Defined activities: Exemption: Harlow District Council 56
Local government: Defined activities: Exemption: Luton Borough Council 56
Local government: Defined activities: Exemption: North Hertfordshire District Council 56
Local government: Defined activities: Exemption: Tunbridge Wells Borough Council 110
Local government: Discretionary payments & injury benefits: Scotland 56
Local government: Discretionary payments: Pensions 118
Local government: Education: Changes: England 110
Local government: England & Wales: Finance 56
Local government: Finance: New parishes 2, 6
Local government: Local authorities: Capital finance 56, 110
Local government: Local authorities: Capital finance: Rate of discount 1998/99 109
Local government: Local authorities: Goods & services 109
Local government: Local authorities: Goods & services: Public bodies 183
Local government: Local authorities: Members' allowances 109, 110
Local government: Local authorities: Transport charges 183
Local government: National Crime Squad Service Authority: Members' interests 184, 187
Local government: National Crime Squad Service Authority: Standing orders 184, 187
Local government: Non-domestic rating: Rural settlements: Wales 8, 120
Local government: Parishes: Isle of Wight 183
Local government: Pension scheme 118
Local government: Pension scheme: Environment Agency 118
Local government: Pension scheme: Scotland 118

Pages 1-23 Jan, 51-69 Feb, 103-131 Mar, 179-196 April

Local government: Public bodies: National Health Service Trusts: Admission to meetings 184
Local government: Public Entertainments Licences (Drug Misuse) Act 1997: Commencement 184
Local government: Registration service: Changes: Berkshire, Cambridgeshire & Cheshire 6
Local government: Registration service: Changes: Devon, Essex, Hereford & Worcester 6
Local government: Registration service: Changes: Kent & Lancashire 6
Local government: Registration service: Changes: Nottinghamshire & Shropshire 6
Local government: Reorganisation: Coroners Act 1988: Amendment 104
Local government: Scottish Legal Services Ombudsman & Commissioner for Local Administration in
Scotland 57
Local government: Staff transfer: Berkshire County Council 109
Local government: Staff transfer: Cambridgeshire County Council: City of Peterborough 109
Local government: Staff transfer: Cheshire County Council: Borough of Halton 109
Local government: Staff transfer: Cheshire County Council: Borough of Warrington 109
Local government: Staff transfer: Devon County Council: Borough of Torbay 109
Local government: Staff transfer: Devon County Council: City of Plymouth 109
Local government: Staff transfer: Essex County Council: Borough of Southend-on-Sea 109
Local government: Staff transfer: Essex County Council: Borough of Thurrock 109
Local government: Staff transfer: Hereford & Worcester 109
Local government: Staff transfer: Kent County Council: Borough of Gillingham 109
Local government: Staff transfer: Kent County Council: City of Rochester 109
Local government: Staff transfer: Lancashire County Council: Borough of Blackburn with Darwen 109
Local government: Staff transfer: Lancashire County Council: Borough of Blackpool 109
Local government: Staff transfer: Nottinghamshire County Council: City of Nottingham 110
Local government: Staff transfer: Shropshire County Council: District of the Wrekin 110
Local government: Superannuation: Scotland 8
Loch Turret, Scotland: Water pollution: Prevention 68
London Borough of Haringey: Trunk roads: Red route: Bus lanes 188
London Borough of Wandsworth: Special parking areas 121
London cabs 179, 185
London Docklands Development Corporation: Designated areas: Alteration 68
London Docklands Development Corporation: Functions: Transfer 130
London Docklands Development Corporation: Property, etc.: Transfer: Lee Valley Regional Park Authority 130
London Docklands Development Corporation: Property, rights & liabilities: Transfer 23
London Docklands Development Corporation: Property, rights & liabilities: Transfer: Urban Regeneration
Agency 130
London government: London traffic control system: Transfer 110
London Residuary Body: Property transfer 106
London traffic control system: Transfer 110
London: East London & the City Health Authority: National Health Service Trust 185
London: Greater London Authority: Referendum 187
Lone parents: Social security 127
Lotteries: Gaming Board: Fees 103
Luton Borough Council: Local government: Defined activities: Exemption 56

M

Mackerel: Prohibition of fishing: Specified sea areas 67
Magistrates' courts: Licensing: Fees 57
Maidstone Borough Council: Local government: Defined activities: Exemption 110
Malaysia: Double taxation relief 5
Mammalian meat & bone meal: Fertilisers 179
Management practice: Codes: Approval: Residential property 5
Marine pollution: Oil preparedness, response & co-operation convention 184
Marriage: Births, deaths, etc.: Fees: Scotland 110, 120
Masters & seamen: Merchant shipping 184
Maternity pay: Statutory: Employers: Compensation 128, 130
Maternity: Suspension from work: Merchant shipping & fishing vessels 195
Meat: Mammalian: Bone meal: Fertilisers 179
Mediation: Family matters: Legal aid 183

Pages 1-23 Jan, 51-69 Feb, 103-131 Mar, 179-196 April

Medical practice: General: Vocational training: National Health Service 111, 114, 117
Medical practice: General: Vocational training: National Health Service: Scotland 7
Medical practitioners: Choice: National Health Service: Scotland 186
Medical profession: National Health Service: General medical practice: Vocational training 111, 114, 117
Medical services: General: National Health Service 114
Medical services: General: National Health Service: Scotland 186
Medicines: Human use: Medical devices: Fees & miscellaneous amendments 111
Medicines: Pharmacy & general sale: Exemption 7
Medicines: Prescription only: Human use 7
Medicines: Sale or supply: Miscellaneous provisions 184
Medicines: Veterinary drugs: Merchants in: Exemptions 184
Medicines: Veterinary medicinal products: Administration: Restrictions 7
Mental nursing homes 187, 195
Merchant shipping & fishing vessels: Maternity: Suspension from work 195
Merchant Shipping Act 1995: Appointed day 7
Merchant shipping: Compulsory insurance: Trans-shipped fish: Ships receiving 57
Merchant shipping: Fees 111
Merchant shipping: Fire protection: Large ships 185
Merchant shipping: Fire protection: Small ships 185
Merchant shipping: Fishing vessels: Crew accommodation 184
Merchant shipping: Fishing vessels: Deck officers & engineer officers 184
Merchant shipping: Fishing vessels: Health & safety at work 7
Merchant shipping: Fishing vessels: Safety provisions 185
Merchant shipping: ISM code: RO-RO passenger ferries 7
Merchant shipping: Light dues 111
Merchant shipping: Oil pollution & general provisions: Guernsey 57
Merchant shipping: Oil pollution: Pitcairn 184
Merchant shipping: Oil pollution: Sovereign base areas 184
Merchant shipping: Oil preparedness, response & co-operation convention 184
Merchant shipping: Pollution: Prevention 57
Merchant shipping: Port waste reception facilities 7
Merchant shipping: Safety 7
Merchant shipping: Safety: Fishing vessels: Life-saving appliances 185
Metropolitan & city police districts: London cabs 179, 185
Mid Glamorgan Ambulance: National Health Service Trust 113
Middlesex Hospital: National Health Service Trust 185
Midwives, health visitors & nurses: Professional conduct 186
Mines: Notice of abandonment 196
Mining: Deep sea: Guernsey 3
Mining: Deep sea: Jersey 3
Ministers of the crown: Secretary of State for the Environment, Transport & the Regions 7
Mink: Keeping 1
Misuse of Drugs Act 1971: Modification 105
Monklands & Bellshill Hospitals: National Health Service Trust 186
Montagu Hospital & Doncaster Royal Infirmary: National Health Service Trust 57
Morecambe Bay Hospitals: National Health Service Trust 113
Motor vehicles: Approval 10
Motor vehicles: Driving licences 10, 121
Motor vehicles: Type approval: Goods vehicles: Great Britain 10
Motor vehicles: Type approval: Great Britain 10
Motorways: A1(M): Blind Lane - Lumley Dene 11
Motorways: A1(M): Burtree interchange to Whitemare Pool 189
Motorways: A1(M): Hatfield Tunnel 61
Motorways: A1(M): Junction 2 189
Motorways: A1(M): Junction 36, Warmsworth 11
Motorways: A1(M): Junction 8, Hertfordshire 189
Motorways: A1(M): Southbound exit slip road, Washington services 61
Motorways: A1(M): Wadworth 66
Motorways: A3(M): Bedhampton - southbound off slip road 121

Pages 1-23 Jan, 51-69 Feb, 103-131 Mar, 179-196 April

ALPHABETICAL INDEX

Motorways: A40(M): Royal Borough of Kensington & Chelsea & Hammersmith & Fulham 13
Motorways: A40(M): Westway, City of Westminster 13
Motorways: A74(M): Central reserve, Greenhillstairs 14
Motorways: A102(M) & A102: Blackwall Tunnel southern approach 125
Motorways: A102(M): East Cross Route, Hackney 125
Motorways: A194(M): Burtree interchange to Whitemare Pool 189
Motorways: A194(M): Whitemare Pool roundabout to Follingsby interchange 15
Motorways: A627(M) 15, 191
Motorways: A627(M): Junction 1, Chadderton roundabout exit slip road 15
Motorways: M1/M18: Thurcroft & Dodworth 17
Motorways: M1: Barnet, Scratchwood railway bridge 16
Motorways: M1: Connecting roads, Leicestershire 192
Motorways: M1: Junction 6 & 8, slip roads 192
Motorways: M1: Junction 11-10 17
Motorways: M1: Junction 19 126
Motorways: M1: Junction 23-23A, Leicestershire 16
Motorways: M1: Junction 24, Leicestershire 16
Motorways: M1: Junction 25, Erewash to Trowell 16
Motorways: M1: Junction 30, Barlborough 16
Motorways: M1: Junction 31, slip roads 17
Motorways: M1: Junction 33-34 192
Motorways: M1: Junction 34 south 17
Motorways: M1: Junction 35A, northbound exit slip road 192
Motorways: M1: Junction 39-40, southbound carriageway 65
Motorways: M1: Junction 40, northbound entry slip road 17
Motorways: M1: Junction 41, slip roads 17
Motorways: M1: Junction 45, southbound entry slip road 17
Motorways: M1: Junction 46 192
Motorways: M1: Leicestershire 16, 65
Motorways: M1: Lofthouse 17
Motorways: M1: Lofthouse interchange 17
Motorways: M1: M1 junction 18 to Watford Gap services, Northamptonshire 16
Motorways: M1: Marker post 26.1 - 32.0 17
Motorways: M1: Marker post 28.0 - 28.7 17
Motorways: M2: Gravesend east 17
Motorways: M2: Junction 3, 5, 6, slip roads 17
Motorways: M2: Marker post 67.4 to 82.3 . . . . 17, 65
Motorways: M3: Junction 5 & 6 17
Motorways: M3: Junction 9 17
Motorways: M3: Junction 13 & 14 17
Motorways: M4: 2nd Severn Crossing, construction access roads 18
Motorways: M4: Brynglas Tunnels, Newport 192
Motorways: M4: Junction 6 8/9 192
Motorways: M4: Junction 7, Eastbound entry slip road 17
Motorways: M4: Junction 12, exit slip roads 17
Motorways: M4: Junction 16-18 192
Motorways: M4: Junction 17-18 126
Motorways: M4: Junction 18, slip roads 17
Motorways: M4: Junction 19-20 126
Motorways: M4: Junction 20/M5 Motorway, junction 15 interchange 126
Motorways: M4: Junction 24-28 192
Motorways: M4: Junction 24-28, Coldra-Tredegar Park, Newport 18
Motorways: M4: Junction 43-46, Llandarcy-Llangyfelach, Neath-Port Talbot & Swansea 18
Motorways: M4: Marker post 61.8 - 59.2 192
Motorways: M4: Membury services westbound, motorway exit slip road 18
Motorways: M4: Westbound exit slip road, junction 42, Earlswood, Neath Port Talbot 18
Motorways: M5: Junction 10 . . . . 65, 126
Motorways: M5: Junction 11 & A40 trunk road: Golden Valley interchange 65
Motorways: M5: Junction 11A-12 65

Pages 1-23 Jan, 51-69 Feb, 103-131 Mar, 179-196 April

Motorways: M5: Junction 12-14 126
Motorways: M5: Junction 12-14, various locations 65
Motorways: M5: Junction 14-15 . . . . 18, 192
Motorways: M5: Junction 2, northbound exit slip road 18
Motorways: M5: Junction 20, slip road 65
Motorways: M5: Junction 21-22 126
Motorways: M5: Junction 22-23 18
Motorways: M5: Junction 25-27 18
Motorways: M5: Junction 4 192
Motorways: M5: Junction 4A, 7 & 8 18
Motorways: M5: Junction 9 . . . . 18, 126
Motorways: M5: Junction 9-10 126
Motorways: M6 126
Motorways: M6: Hackthorpe Bridge 18
Motorways: M6: Junction 3-2 18
Motorways: M6: Junction 5 northbound exit slip road 18
Motorways: M6: Junction 6, Gravelly Hill, slip roads 18
Motorways: M6: Junction 11, slip roads 192
Motorways: M6: Junction 15-14 192
Motorways: M6: Junction 15-16 19
Motorways: M6: Junction 18-19 19
Motorways: M6: Junction 19 126
Motorways: M6: Junction 20, link roads 18
Motorways: M6: Junction 20, northbound entry slip road, Lymm interchange 65
Motorways: M6: Junction 20, northbound exit slip road 18
Motorways: M6: Junction 21A, Croft, link roads 65
Motorways: M6: Junction 22-21 19
Motorways: M6: Junction 24, northbound entry slip road 18
Motorways: M6: Junction 27 & 28 192
Motorways: M6: Junction 28, southbound exit slip road 192
Motorways: M6: Junction 32 - 33 192
Motorways: M6: Junction 32, southbound carriageway 65
Motorways: M6: Junction 34 & slip roads 192
Motorways: M6: Junction 34, slip roads 66
Motorways: M6: Junction 36 18
Motorways: M6: M56 link road, Lymm interchange 65
Motorways: M6: Sandwell, West Midlands 192
Motorways: M6: Saredon & Packington diversions 55
Motorways: M6: Staffordshire bridges 18
Motorways: M8/A8: Newhouse to St James, slip roads 19
Motorways: M8: Junction 5, slip roads 66
Motorways: M8: Junction 8, Baillieston to junction 29, St James 19
Motorways: M10: Junction 1 to M1, junction 7 66
Motorways: M11: Junction 4, northbound entry slip road 193
Motorways: M11: Junction 4-6 193
Motorways: M11: Junction 6 192
Motorways: M11: Junction 7, northbound exit slip road 66
Motorways: M11: Junction 8, Birchanger roundabout 19
Motorways: M11: Junction 8-9 19
Motorways: M11: Junction 11-12 19
Motorways: M11: Junction 27, Theydon link 19
Motorways: M11: M25 junction 27, northbound M11 to westbound M25 66
Motorways: M11: Marker post 22.9 - 30.6 193
Motorways: M11: Stansted rail bridge, Essex 19
Motorways: M18/M1: Thurcroft & Dodworth 17
Motorways: M18: Junction 2-3 19
Motorways: M18: Langham interchange 19
Motorways: M18: North Ings 19
Motorways: M18: Thurcroft 66

Pages 1-23 Jan, 51-69 Feb, 103-131 Mar, 179-196 April

ALPHABETICAL INDEX

Motorways: M18: Wadworth 66, 193
Motorways: M20: Marker post 85.5 - 89.5 126
Motorways: M20: Marker post 99.10 - 109.60 193
Motorways: M20: Round Hill Tunnel 66
Motorways: M20: Swanley interchange 19
Motorways: M23: Junction 8, southbound exit slip road 66
Motorways: M23: Marker post 30.0 - 37.3 193
Motorways: M25: Bell Common Tunnel 66
Motorways: M25: Holmesdale tunnel 19, 66
Motorways: M25: Junction 2 66
Motorways: M25: Junction 18 193
Motorways: M25: Junction 18, eastbound slip roads 19
Motorways: M25: Junction 19 193
Motorways: M25: Junction 19-18 193
Motorways: M25: Junction 27, Theydon link 19
Motorways: M25: Junction 29 193
Motorways: M25: Junction 30 19
Motorways: M25: Link road 192
Motorways: M25: M25 junction 27, northbound M11 to westbound M25 66
Motorways: M25: Marker post 125.0 - 133.0 19
Motorways: M25: Marker post 132.70 - 139.60 193
Motorways: M25: Swanley interchange 19
Motorways: M27: Junction 1-2 20
Motorways: M27: Junction 12, Portsbridge 19
Motorways: M42 18
Motorways: M42: Catshill interchange, Bromsgrove 66
Motorways: M42: Dunton diversion 55
Motorways: M42: Junction 7a-8, Warwickshire 20
Motorways: M42: Junction 9-10, Warwickshire 20
Motorways: M45: M1 junction 18 to Watford Gap services, Northamptonshire 16
Motorways: M50: Hereford & Worcester 193
Motorways: M50: Junction 4 125
Motorways: M50: Ross Spur 20
Motorways: M53: Junction 1, Bidston Moss viaduct 20
Motorways: M53: Junction 2, northbound entry slip road 20
Motorways: M53: Junction 8-11 20
Motorways: M53: Junction 11, Birkenhead to Manchester link road 193
Motorways: M55: Junction 3-1 127
Motorways: M56: Bridgeworks 20
Motorways: M56: Junction 1-3 20
Motorways: M56. Junction 3-2, eastbound carriageway 20
Motorways: M56: Junction 5, eastbound exit slip road 127
Motorways: M56: Junction 6 & the eastbound entry slip road 20
Motorways: M56: Junction 9, Chester to Birmingham link road 66, 193
Motorways: M56: Junction 15, Manchester to Chester link road 193
Motorways: M56: Link road junction 15 20
Motorways: M56: M6 link road, Lymm interchange 65
Motorways: M56: Westbound link road to M6 northbound carriageway & A50, Lymm interchange 66
Motorways: M58: Junction 5, slip roads 193
Motorways: M61: And link roads 20
Motorways: M61: Bridgeworks 193
Motorways: M61: Junction 4 - 3 66
Motorways: M61: Sandhole Loop Bridge 193
Motorways: M61: Southbound carriageway 193
Motorways: M62 21
Motorways: M62: Junction 9 194
Motorways: M62: Junction 9, 11-12 & slip roads 20
Motorways: M62: Junction 11-12 20
Motorways: M62: Junction 12, Eccles interchange & link roads 20

Pages 1-23 Jan, 51-69 Feb, 103-131 Mar, 179-196 April

Motorways: M62: Junction 13, eastbound entry slip road 194
Motorways: M62: Junction 13, eastbound exit slip road 20
Motorways: M62: Junction 13, westbound access slip road 20
Motorways: M62: Junction 14, slip roads 127
Motorways: M62: Junction 18 194
Motorways: M62: Junction 19-18 127
Motorways: M62: Junction 20, eastbound exit slip road 20
Motorways: M62: Junction 21, westbound exit slip road 127
Motorways: M62: Junction 23, eastbound exit slip road 66
Motorways: M62: Junction 24-25 20
Motorways: M62: Junction 26 & 27 17
Motorways: M62: Junction 32-33 194
Motorways: M62: Junction 35-36 194
Motorways: M62: Junction 37, Howden 66
Motorways: M62: Lofthouse interchange 17
Motorways: M62: Slip roads 194
Motorways: M62: Westbound exit slip road, Hartshead service area 20
Motorways: M63 21
Motorways: M63: Bridgeworks 20
Motorways: M63: Junction 3 194
Motorways: M63: Junction 3 & 4, slip roads 21
Motorways: M63: Junction 3, northbound exit slip road 66
Motorways: M63: Junction 3, slip roads 66
Motorways: M63: Junction 3, southbound access slip road 66
Motorways: M63: Junction 3, southbound exit slip road 127
Motorways: M63: Junction 8-9 21
Motorways: M63: Junction 9, northbound access slip road 21
Motorways: M63: Junction 9, northbound carriageway 67
Motorways: M63: Junction 10, slip road 20
Motorways: M63: Junction 10, southbound exit slip road 21
Motorways: M65: Junction 6-7, & slip roads 21
Motorways: M66: Junction 0-1, southbound carriageway 21
Motorways: M66: Junction 1, 3 & 4 slip roads 194
Motorways: M66: Junction 3, northbound exit slip road 67
Motorways: M66: Junction 3, southbound access slip road 21
Motorways: M66: Junction 4 . . . . 21, 194
Motorways: M66: Junction 4, southbound exit slip road 67
Motorways: M66: Slip roads 194
Motorways: M67: Junction 1 & 3, slip roads 67
Motorways: M67: Junction 3 194
Motorways: M67: Major bridgeworks 21
Motorways: M69: Connecting roads, Leicestershire 192
Motorways: M69: Leicestershire 16, 65
Motorways: M73: Northbound carriageway from junction 2, Baillieston to junction 3, Mollinsburn 21
Motorways: M73: Slip road to northbound M74 at junction 1, Maryville 21
Motorways: M74: Junction 3, Daldowie 21
Motorways: M180: Junction 3-4 194
Motorways: M602 21
Motorways: M602: Junction 2 21
Motorways: M602: Junction 2 & 3 194
Motorways: M602: Junction 3-2 194
Motorways: M602: Westbound link road to M62 21
Motorways: M621: Gildersome 17
Motorways: M621: Junction 1 & 2, slip roads 67
Museums & Galleries Act 1992: Amendment 111
Museums & galleries: Northern Ireland 58

Pages 1-23 Jan, 51-69 Feb, 103-131 Mar, 179-196 April

N

National assistance: Assessment of resources 111
National assistance: Personal requirements: Sums 111
National Crime Squad Service Authority: Members' interests 184, 187
National Crime Squad Service Authority: Standing orders 184, 187
National Crime Squad: Complaints 118
National Crime Squad: Discipline: Senior police members 118
National Crime Squad: Secretary of State's objectives 58
National Crime Squad: Senior police members: Appeals 118
National Health Service (Primary Care) Act 1997: Commencement 114
National Health Service Trusts: Ashford & St. Peter's Hospitals 111, 112
National Health Service Trusts: Bay Community 111
National Health Service Trusts: Bishop Auckland Hospitals 111
National Health Service Trusts: Canterbury & Thanet Community Healthcare 111
National Health Service Trusts: Cheviot & Wansbeck, North Tyneside Health Care 112
National Health Service Trusts: Chichester Priority Care Services 57
National Health Service Trusts: Community Health Care: North Durham 185
National Health Service Trusts: Crawley Horsham 112
National Health Service Trusts: Darlington Memorial Hospital 112
National Health Service Trusts: Derby City General Hospital 112
National Health Service Trusts: Derbyshire Royal Infirmary 112
National Health Service Trusts: Doncaster Royal Infirmary & Montagu Hospital 57
National Health Service Trusts: Durham County Priority Services 112
National Health Service Trusts: East London & the City Health Authority 185
National Health Service Trusts: East Surrey Healthcare 112
National Health Service Trusts: East Surrey Priority Care 112
National Health Service Trusts: Freeman Group of Hospitals 112
National Health Service Trusts: Frenchay Healthcare 57
National Health Service Trusts: Furness Hospitals 112
National Health Service Trusts: Gateshead Health 113
National Health Service Trusts: Gateshead Healthcare 113
National Health Service Trusts: Gateshead Hospitals 113
National Health Service Trusts: Glan Hafren 113
National Health Service Trusts: Glan-y-Môr 113
National Health Service Trusts: Hairmyres & Stonehouse Hospitals 185
National Health Service Trusts: Heathlands Mental Health 112
National Health Service Trusts: Horton General Hospital 113
National Health Service Trusts: Isle of Wight Healthcare 57
National Health Service Trusts: Lancaster Acute Hospitals 113
National Health Service Trusts: Lancaster Priority Services 113
National Health Service Trusts: Law Hospital 185
National Health Service Trusts: Leeds Community & Mental Health Services Teaching . . 57
National Health Service Trusts: Leeds Teaching Hospitals 113
National Health Service Trusts: Lewisham & Guy's Mental Health 185
National Health Service Trusts: Lifespan Health Care Cambridge 185
National Health Service Trusts: Lincoln District Healthcare 57
National Health Service Trusts: Lincolnshire Ambulance & Health Transport Service . . 185
National Health Service Trusts: Llandough Hospital & Community 116
National Health Service Trusts: Mid Glamorgan Ambulance 113
National Health Service Trusts: Middlesex Hospital 185
National Health Service Trusts: Monklands & Bellshill Hospitals 186
National Health Service Trusts: Morecambe Bay Hospitals 113
National Health Service Trusts: Newcastle upon Tyne Hospitals 114
National Health Service Trusts: North Downs Community Health 112
National Health Service Trusts: North Durham Acute Hospitals 114
National Health Service Trusts: North Durham Health Care 115
National Health Service Trusts: North Kent Healthcare 112
National Health Service Trusts: North Wales Ambulance 115

Pages 1-23 Jan, 51-69 Feb, 103-131 Mar, 179-196 April

National Health Service Trusts: North Warwickshire 115
National Health Service Trusts: Northallerton Health Services 57
National Health Service Trusts: Northumberland Community Health 112
National Health Service Trusts: Northumbria Health Care 115
National Health Service Trusts: Northwick Park & St Mark's 115
National Health Service Trusts: Public bodies: Admission to meetings 184
National Health Service Trusts: Rhondda Health Care 115
National Health Service Trusts: Royal Brompton & Harefield Hospitals 112, 115
National Health Service Trusts: Royal Victoria Infirmary & Associated Hospitals 112
National Health Service Trusts: Rugby 115
National Health Service Trusts: Shropshire's Community & Mental Health Services 115
National Health Service Trusts: Shropshire's Community Health Service 115
National Health Service Trusts: Shropshire's Mental Health 115
National Health Service Trusts: South & East Wales Ambulance 115
National Health Service Trusts: South Cumbria Community & Mental Health 115
National Health Service Trusts: South Durham 115
National Health Service Trusts: South Durham Health Care 115
National Health Service Trusts: South Kent Community Healthcare 116
National Health Service Trusts: South Warwickshire Combined Care 116
National Health Service Trusts: South Warwickshire Health Care 112
National Health Service Trusts: South Warwickshire Mental Health 112
National Health Service Trusts: Southern Derbyshire Acute Hospitals 115
National Health Service Trusts: St. James & Seacroft University Hospitals 116
National Health Service Trusts: Surrey & Sussex Healthcare 116
National Health Service Trusts: Surrey Hampshire Borders 116
National Health Service Trusts: Surrey Heartlands 112
National Health Service Trusts: Surrey Oaklands 116
National Health Service Trusts: Thames Gateway 116
National Health Service Trusts: Thameslink Healthcare 112
National Health Service Trusts: United Leeds Teaching Hospitals 116
National Health Service Trusts: University College Hospital: Special trustees 185
National Health Service Trusts: Walsgrave Hospitals 116
National Health Service Trusts: Welsh Ambulance Services 116
National Health Service Trusts: West Wales Ambulance 116
National Health Service Trusts: Westminster & Roehampton Hospitals: Special trustees 116
National Health Service Trusts: Westmorland Hospitals 116
National Health Service: Choice of medical practitioner: Scotland 186
National Health Service: Dental charges 113
National Health Service: Dental charges: Scotland 117
National Health Service: Drugs & appliances: Charges 113
National Health Service: Drugs & appliances: Charges: Scotland 116
National Health Service: Fund-holding practices 113
National Health Service: Fund-holding practices: Scotland 186
National Health Service: General medical practice: Vocational training 111, 114, 117
National Health Service: General medical practice: Vocational training: Scotland 7
National Health Service: General medical services 114
National Health Service: General medical services: Scotland 7, 186
National Health Service: Health authorities: Functions: Prescribing incentive schemes 113
National Health Service: Injury benefits 114
National Health Service: Medical practitioner: Choice 113
National Health Service: North & East Devon Health Authority 57
National Health Service: Optical charges & payments 114
National Health Service: Optical charges & payments: Scotland 117
National Health Service: Originating capital debt 114
National Health Service: Originating capital debt: Wales 114
National Health Service: Overseas visitors: Charges: Scotland 57
National Health Service: Pension scheme 114
National Health Service: Pharmaceutical services 114
National Health Service: Pilot schemes 103, 114, 117, 127, 130

Pages 1-23 Jan, 51-69 Feb, 103-131 Mar, 179-196 April

National Health Service: Pilot schemes 7
National Health Service: Pilot schemes: Practitioners 114, 117
National Health Service: Pilot schemes: Proposals & miscellaneous amendments 7
National Health Service: Remuneration & conditions of service 114
National Health Service: Service committees & tribunal 114
National Health Service: Service committees & tribunal: Scotland 186
National Heritage Act 1997: Commencement 58
National Insurance Fund: Payments: Social security 128
National radio multiplex revenue: Percentage 51
Natural habitats: Conservation 2, 23
Naval, military & air forces etc.: Disablement & death: Service pensions 58
Navigation services charges: Civil aviation 104
NCIS Service Authority: Provisions: Police Act 1997 119
NCIS: Complaints 118
NCIS: Discipline: Senior police members 118
NCIS: Secretary of State's objectives 58
NCIS: Senior police members: Appeals 118
New deal: Social security: Miscellaneous provisions 67
Newcastle upon Tyne Hospitals: National Health Service Trust 114
Nitrate sensitive areas 51
Non-automatic weighing instruments: EEC requirements 23
Non-domestic rating & council tax: Demand notices: Rural rate relief: England 2, 8
Non-domestic rating: Contributions: Wales 8
Non-domestic rating: Demand notices: Rural rate relief: Wales 59
Non-domestic rating: Rural areas & rateable value limits: Scotland 8
Non-domestic rating: Rural settlements: England 119
Non-domestic rating: Rural settlements: Local government: Wales 8, 120
Non-domestic rating: Scotland 59
North & East Devon Health Authority: National Health Service 57
North American Gateway Ltd.: Public telecommunication systems 129
North Downs Community Health: National Health Service Trust 112
North Durham Acute Hospitals: National Health Service Trust 114
North Durham Health Care: National Health Service Trust 115
North Durham: Community Health Care: National Health Service Trust 185
North Hertfordshire District Council: Local government: Defined activities: Exemption 56
North Kent Healthcare: National Health Service Trust 112
North Tyneside Health Care, Cheviot & Wansbeck: National Health Service Trust 112
North Wales Ambulance: National Health Service Trust 115
North Wales: Combined probation areas 8
North Warwickshire: National Health Service Trust 115
Northallerton Health Services: National Health Service Trust 57
Northern Ireland (Emergency Provisions) Act 1996: Code of practice 58
Northern Ireland (Emergency Provisions) Act 1996: Interviews: Silent video recording of 58
Northern Ireland (Entry to Negotiations, etc) Act 1996: Section 3: Cessation 186
Northern Ireland Arms Decommissioning Act 1997: Amnesty period 186
Northern Ireland: Appropriation 117
Northern Ireland: Civil evidence 8
Northern Ireland: Criminal Procedure & Investigations Act 1996: Appointed day 3
Northern Ireland: Criminal Procedure & Investigations Act 1996: Code of Practice 3
Northern Ireland: Deregulation 8
Northern Ireland: Education: Student loans 58
Northern Ireland: Financial provisions 117
Northern Ireland: Housing accomodation & homelessness 182
Northern Ireland: Knives: Forfeited property 53
Northern Ireland: Museums & galleries 58
Northern Ireland: Negotiations: Referendum 186
Northern Ireland: Public order: Forms 117
Northern Ireland: Public Processions (Northern Ireland) Act 1998: Commencement 117
Northern Ireland: Public processions: Code of conduct 117

Northern Ireland: Public processions: Guidelines 117
Northern Ireland: Public processions: Notice: Exceptions 186
Northern Ireland: Public processions: Procedural rules 117
Northumberland Community Health: National Health Service Trust 112
Northumbria Health Care: National Health Service Trust 115
Northwick Park & St Mark's: National Health Service Trust 115
Nottinghamshire County Council: City of Nottingham: Local government: Staff transfer 110
Nottinghamshire: Coroners 52
Nursery education: England 106
Nurses, midwives & health visitors: Professional conduct 186
Nursing homes 187, 195
Nursing homes: Registration: Scotland 119

O

Occupational & personal pension schemes: Levy & register 118
Offshore installations: Safety zones 117
Offshore petroleum: Production & pipelines: Environmental effects: Assessment 187
Oil pollution & general provisions: Merchant shipping: Guernsey 57
Oil pollution: Merchant shipping: Pitcairn 184
Oil pollution: Merchant shipping: Sovereign base areas 184
Optical charges & payments: National Health Service 114
Optical charges & payments: National Health Service: Scotland 117
Optical Council: General: Registration & enrolment: Rules 8
Opticians: General Optical Council: Registration & enrolment: Rules 8
OSPAR Commission: Immunities & privileges 6
Osteopaths Act 1993: Commencement orders 117
Osteopaths: General Osteopathic Council: Conditional registration 186
Osteopaths: General Osteopathic Council: Constitution & procedure 186
Osteopaths: General Osteopathic Council: Transitional period: Registration & fees: Application 186
Overseas visitors: Charges: National Health Service: Scotland 57

P

Parents: Lone: Social security 127
Parishes & communities: Local elections 120
Parishes: Isle of Wight 183
Parishes: New: Local government: Finance 2, 6
Parking area: Special: Royal Borough of Kingston upon Thames 60
Pedestrian crossings: Pelican & puffin 188
Pelican pedestrian crossings 188
Pensions: Environment Agency: Local government scheme 118
Pensions: Firemen 182
Pensions: Guaranteed minimum increase 118
Pensions: Increase: Review 118
Pensions: Local government: Discretionary payments 118
Pensions: Local government: Pension scheme 118
Pensions: Local government: Pension scheme: Scotland 118
Pensions: Local government: Superannuation: Scotland 8
Pensions: Money purchase contracted-out schemes: Reduced rates & rebates 187
Pensions: National Health Service: Pension scheme 114
Pensions: Naval, military & air forces, etc.: Disablement & death 58
Pensions: Occupational & personal pension schemes: Levy & register 118
Pensions: Personal injuries: Civilians 58
Pensions: Police 119
Pensions: Superannuation Act 1972: Admission 118
Pensions: Teachers 4
Personal injuries: Civilians 58
Personal pension schemes: Minimum contributions 187

Pages 1-23 Jan, 51-69 Feb, 103-131 Mar, 179-196 April

Peterborough: Coroners 52
Petroleum: Offshore: Production & pipelines: Environmental effects: Assessment 187
Petty sessional divisions 6
Pharmaceutical services: National Health Service 114
Pharmacy: Exemption: Medicines: Sale 7
Phone Company: Public telecommunication systems 68
Pipe-lines: Offshore petroleum: Production: Environtmental effects: Assessment 187
Pistachios: From Iran: Emergency control 5
Pitcairn: Oil pollution: Merchant shipping 184
Place of supply of services: Value added tax 195
Plaice: Prohibition of fishing: Specified sea areas 67
Plant health 118
Plant health: Great Britain 8
Plants: Health: Potatoes: Originating in: Egypt 58
Police 119
Police Act 1997: Commencement & transitional provisions 119
Police Act 1997: NCIS Service Authority: Provisions 119
Police Information Technology Organisation: Additional bodies 119
Police: Grant: Scotland 187
Police: National Crime Squad Service Authority: Members' interests 184, 187
Police: National Crime Squad Service Authority: Standing orders 184, 187
Police: National Crime Squad: Complaints 118
Police: National Crime Squad: Discipline: Senior police members 118
Police: National Crime Squad: Secretary of State's objectives 58
Police: National Crime Squad: Senior police members: Appeals 118
Police: NCIS: Complaints 118
Police: NCIS: Discipline: Senior police members 118
Police: NCIS: Secretary of State's objectives 58
Police: NCIS: Senior police members: Appeals 118
Police: Pensions 119
Police: Scotland 187
Police: Secretary of State's objectives 58
Pollution: Prevention: Merchant shipping 57
Port of Birkenhead Harbour: Empowerment 182
Porthmadog Harbour revision 107
Potato marketing scheme: Certification of revocation 1
Potatoes: Originating in: Eygpt 58
Prescription only medicines: Human use 7
Prevention of Terrorism (Temporary Provisions) Act 1989: Partial continuance 119
Primetec (UK) Ltd.: Public telecommunication systems 129
Principal areas: Local elections 120
Prisons: Rules 8
Probation: Combined areas 8, 119
Proceeds of Crime (Scotland) Act 1995: Northern Ireland Orders: Enforcement 180
Prosecutors: Prescription: Pre-sentence report: Disclosure 53
Public bodies: Admission to meetings: National Health Service Trusts 184
Public bodies: Local authorities: Goods & services 109, 183
Public Entertainments Licences (Drug Misuse) Act 1997: Commencement 184
Public health: Contamination of food 58, 59, 119
Public health: Nursing homes: Registration: Scotland 119
Public health: Residential care homes: Nursing homes & mental nursing homes 187, 195
Public order: Forms: Northern Ireland 117
Public Processions (Northern Ireland) Act 1998: Code of conduct 117
Public Processions (Northern Ireland) Act 1998: Commencement 117
Public Processions (Northern Ireland) Act 1998: Guidelines 117
Public Processions (Northern Ireland) Act 1998: Procedural rules 117
Public processions: Notice: Exceptions: Northern Ireland 186
Public Record Office: Fees 187
Public telecommunication systems: Atlantic Telecommunications Ltd. 129

Pages 1-23 Jan, 51-69 Feb, 103-131 Mar, 179-196 April

Public telecommunication systems: AXS Telecom (UK) Ltd. 67
Public telecommunication systems: Easynet Group Plc 129
Public telecommunication systems: Esprit Telecom UK Ltd. 129
Public telecommunication systems: Eurobell (Holdings) Plc. 67
Public telecommunication systems: Frontel Communications Ltd. 67
Public telecommunication systems: GT UK Ltd. 67
Public telecommunication systems: HighwayOne Corporation Ltd. 68
Public telecommunication systems: IDT Global Ltd. 68
Public telecommunication systems: Internet Network Services Ltd. 68
Public telecommunication systems: Izencom Ltd. 68
Public telecommunication systems: KDD Europe Ltd. 68
Public telecommunication systems: LCI Telecom UK Ltd. 129
Public telecommunication systems: North American Gateway Ltd. 129
Public telecommunication systems: Primetec (UK) Ltd. 129
Public telecommunication systems: Shropshire Cable & Telecoms Ltd. 22
Public telecommunication systems: Skylight Holdings Inc. 68
Public telecommunication systems: Sonic Telecommunications International Ltd. 129
Public telecommunication systems: Sussex Cable & Telecoms Ltd. 22
Public telecommunication systems: Telecom Ireland Ltd. 129
Public telecommunication systems: Telegroup UK Ltd. 129
Public telecommunication systems: Teleport (Northern Ireland) Ltd. 68
Public telecommunication systems: TGC UK Ltd. 129
Public telecommunication systems: The Phone Company 68
Puffin pedestrian crossings 188
Pupils: Individual: Achievements: Information 181
Pyx: Trial of 52

R

Radioactivity in sheep: Food protection 58, 59
Railways: Rateable values: Scotland 187
Rates: Non-domestic: Levying: Scotland 119
Rating & valuation: Council tax & non-domestic rating: Demand notices: Rural relief: England 2, 8
Rating & valuation: Exempted classes: Scotland 120
Rating & valuation: Non-domestic rating: Contributions: Wales 8
Rating & valuation: Non-domestic rating: Demand notices: Rural rate relief: Wales 59
Rating & valuation: Non-domestic rating: Rural areas & rateable value limits: Scotland 8
Rating & valuation: Non-domestic rating: Rural settlements: England 119
Rating & valuation: Non-domestic rating: Rural settlements: Wales 8, 120
Rating & valuation: Non-domestic rating: Scotland 59, 119
Rating & valuation: Railways: Scotland 187
Rating & valuation: Rating lists: Valuation date 8
Rating lists: Valuation date 8
Rating: Re-rating: Social security 128
Recreational craft 52
Referendum: Greater London Authority 187
Referendum: Negotiations: Northern Ireland 186
Registration of births, deaths, marriages, etc.: Adopted persons: Contact register: Fees 120
Registration of births, deaths, marriages, etc.: Fees: Scotland 110, 120
Relocation grants: Form of application 108
Rent Act registration areas: Local government: Changes 6
Representation of the people: European Parliamentary elections: Day of by-election: Yorkshire South constituency 120
Representation of the people: Local elections: Parishes & communities 120
Representation of the people: Local elections: Principal areas 120
Residential care homes 187, 195
Residential property: Management practice: Codes: Approval 5
Restrictive trade practices: Non-notifiable agreements: Sale & purchase, share subscription & franchise agreements 9

ALPHABETICAL INDEX

Restrictive trade practices: Non-notifiable agreements: Turnover threshold 9
Retirement benefits schemes: Discretion to approve: Restriction 108
Retirement benefits schemes: Earnings cap: Indexation 108
Revenue traders: Accounts & records 3
Rhondda Health Care: National Health Service Trust 115
River Ewe Salmon Fishery District: Baits & lures 120
River Nene: Bridge: Scheme 182
River Tweed: Baits & lures 9
River, Scotland: Salmon & freshwater fisheries: River Ewe: Baits & lures 120
River, Scotland: Salmon & freshwater fisheries: River Tweed: Baits & lures 9
Ro-Ro passenger ferries: ISM code: Merchant shipping 7
Road Traffic Act 1991: Commencement 188
Road traffic: A10: Haringey: Red route 9
Road traffic: A1: Haringey: Red route 9
Road traffic: A1: Islington: Red route: Experimental 59
Road traffic: A205: Greenwich: Red route 121
Road traffic: A205: Greenwich: Red route: Banned turns 9
Road traffic: A205: Greenwich: Red route: Experimental 188
Road traffic: A205: Lambeth: Red route: Experimental 121
Road traffic: A205: Lewisham: Red route: Experimental 9
Road traffic: A205: Southwark: Red route: Bus lanes: Experimental 9
Road traffic: A205: Southwark: Red route: Experimental 9, 59
Road traffic: A23: Lambeth: Red route: Experimental 9
Road traffic: A23: Lambeth: Red route: Prohibition of traffic 59
Road traffic: A316: Richmond: Red route 9
Road traffic: A3: Kingston & Wandsworth 59
Road traffic: A406: Hanger Lane & Ashbourne Rd., Ealing 59
Road traffic: A40: Western Ave., Ealing: Speed limits 120
Road traffic: A41: Camden: Red route: Bus lanes 120
Road traffic: A41: Camden: Temporary prohibition of traffic 9
Road traffic: A41: Westminster: Red route 59, 188
Road traffic: A4: Bath Rd. & Hatch Lane, Hillingdon 120
Road traffic: A4: Bath Rd. & Newport Rd., Hillingdon 120
Road traffic: A4: Colnbrook bypass, Hillingdon 120
Road traffic: A4: Colnbrook bypass, Tarmac Way & Stanwell Moor Rd., Hillingdon 120
Road traffic: A501: Camden & Westminster: Red route 60
Road traffic: A501: Euston Rd., Camden: Red route: Prescribed routes 10
Road traffic: Finance Act 1997: Commencement 121
Road traffic: London Borough of Haringey: Trunk roads: Red route: Bus lanes 188
Road traffic: London Borough of Wandsworth: Special parking areas 121
Road traffic: Motor vehicles: Approval 10
Road traffic: Motor vehicles: Driving licences 10, 121
Road traffic: Motor vehicles: Type approval: Goods vehicles: Great Britain 10
Road traffic: Motor vehicles: Type approval: Great Britain 10
Road traffic: Pedestrian crossings: Pelican & puffin 188
Road traffic: Road vehicles: Construction & use 10
Road traffic: Road vehicles: Registration: Fee 121, 188
Road traffic: Road vehicles: Statutory off-road notification 60
Road traffic: Special parking area: London Borough of Bromley 10
Road traffic: Special parking area: London Borough of Haringey 10
Road traffic: Special parking area: Royal Borough of Kingston upon Thames 60
Road traffic: Speed limits 10, 11, 60, 188
Road traffic: Traffic regulation 11, 12, 13, 14, 15, 16, 17, 18, 19,
. . . . 20, 21, 60, 61, 62, 63, 64, 65, 66, 67, 121, 122, 123,
. . . . 124, 125, 126, 127, 188, 189, 190, 191, 192, 193, 194
Road traffic: Traffic signs: Temporary obstructions 10
Road traffic: Traffic signs: Temporary: Prescribed bodies: England & Wales 10
Road traffic: Trunk roads: A12: Redbridge: Red route 9
Road traffic: Trunk roads: A23: Croydon: Red route 9

Pages 1-23 Jan, 51-69 Feb, 103-131 Mar, 179-196 April

Road traffic: Trunk roads: A41: Camden 188
Road traffic: Trunk roads: A205: Lambeth: Red route 188
Road traffic: Trunk roads: A205: Lewisham: Bus lanes: Red route 188
Road traffic: Trunk roads: A1400: Redbridge: Red route 10
Road traffic: Trunk roads: London Borough of Lambeth: Red route: Bus lanes 60
Road traffic: Vehicle emissions: Fixed penalty 10
Road traffic: Vehicle excise duty: Immobilisation, removal & disposal of vehicles 10
Road vehicles: Construction & use 10
Road vehicles: Registration: Fee 121, 188
Road vehicles: Statutory off-road notification 60
Road works: Inspection fees: Scotland 188
Roads & bridges: Road works: Inspection fees: Scotland 188
Roads & bridges: Scotland 59, 188
Roads & bridges: Scotland: Special roads 188
Roehampton & Westminster Hospitals: Special trustees: National Health Service Trust 116
Royal Borough of Kingston upon Thames: Special parking area 60
Royal Brompton & Harefield: National Health Service Trust 115
Royal Brompton Hospital: National Health Service Trust 112
Royal Victoria Infirmary & Associated Hospitals: National Health Service Trust 112
Rugby: National Health Service Trust 115
Rural areas & rateable value limits: Non-domestic rating: Scotland 8
Rural rate relief: Non-domestic rating: Demand notices: Wales 59
Rural settlements: Non-domestic rating: England 119
Rutland: Combined probation areas 119

S

Safety zones: Offshore installations 117
Salisbury District Council: Local government: Defined activities: Exemption 110
Salmon & freshwater fisheries: River Ewe: Baits & lures 120
School teachers: Pay & conditions 181
Schools: Direct grant 4
Schools: Grant-maintained & grant-maintained special 181
Schools: Grant-maintained & grant-maintained special schools: Finance: Wales 105
Schools: Grant-maintained: New: Finance 181
Schools: Independent: Special educational needs: Approval 106
Scotland: Act of Sederunt: Court of Session: Rules: Solicitors & notaries public 2
Scotland: Advice & assistance: Financial conditions 183
Scotland: Advice & assistance: Representation 6
Scotland: Area tourist boards: Amending scheme 110
Scotland: Civil legal aid 183
Scotland: Civil legal aid: Financial conditions 183
Scotland: Council tax: Discounts 104
Scotland: Council tax: Exempt dwellings 104
Scotland: Court of Session: Rules: Shorthand writers: Fees 180
Scotland: Criminal legal aid: Prescribed proceedings 6
Scotland: Environment Act 1995: Commencement 181
Scotland: General medical services: National Health Service 186
Scotland: Homeless persons: Priority need 5
Scotland: Housing Grants, Construction & Regeneration Act 1996: Commencement 180
Scotland: Housing Revenue Account General Fund: Contribution limits 56
Scotland: Housing support grant 182
Scotland: Legal aid & advice 183
Scotland: Local government: Discretionary payments & injury benefits 56
Scotland: Local government: Pension scheme 118
Scotland: Local government: Superannuation 8
Scotland: Loch Turret: Water pollution: Prevention 68
Scotland: National Health Service: Choice of medical practitioner 186
Scotland: National Health Service: Dental charges 117

ALPHABETICAL INDEX

Scotland: National Health Service: Drugs & appliances: Charges 116
Scotland: National Health Service: Fund-holding practices 186
Scotland: National Health Service: General medical practice: Vocational training 7
Scotland: National Health Service: General medical services 7
Scotland: National Health Service: Optical charges & payments 117
Scotland: National Health Service: Overseas visitors: Charges 57
Scotland: National Health Service: Service committees & tribunal 186
Scotland: Non-domestic rates: Levying 119
Scotland: Non-domestic rating 59
Scotland: Non-domestic rating: Rural areas & rateable value limits 8
Scotland: Nursing homes: Registration 119
Scotland: Police 187
Scotland: Police: Grant 187
Scotland: Proceeds of crime: Northern Ireland Orders: Enforcement 180
Scotland: Railways: Rateable values 187
Scotland: Rating & valuation: Exempted classes 120
Scotland: Registration of births, deaths, marriages, etc.: Fees 110, 120
Scotland: Road works: Inspection fees 188
Scotland: Scottish Legal Services Ombudsman & Commissioner for Local Administration in Scotland 57
Scotland: Sewerage: Domestic charges: Reduction 131
Scotland: Surface waters: Dangerous substances: Classification 69
Scotland: Teachers: Premature retirement & redundancy: Compensation 181
Scotland: Teachers: Superannuation 181
Scotland: Town & country planning: General permitted development 22
Scotland: Town & country planning: Use classes 23
Scotland: Water services: Billing & collection: Reduction 131
Scottish Legal Services Ombudsman & Commissioner for Local Administration in Scotland 57
Sea fisheries 67
Sea fisheries: Community quota measures: Enforcement 127
Sea fisheries: Conservation of sea fish 67
Sea fisheries: Conservation: Seals: Shetland Islands area 194
Sea fisheries: Third country fishing: Enforcement 127
Sea fishing: Community quota measures: Enforcement 127
Seals: Conservation: Shetland Islands area 194
Secretary of State for the Environment, Transport & the Regions 7
Secure training centre: Escorts: Rules 127
Secure training centres: Criminal Justice & Public Order Act 1994: Custody Officer certificate: Suspension 127
Secure training centres: Rules 127
Sentencing: Crime: Pre-sentence report: Disclosure: Prosecutors: Prescription 53
Sewerage: Domestic charges: Reduction: Scotland 131
Sheep: Annual premium: Quotas 1
Sheep: Radioactivity: Food protection 58, 59
Shellfish: Live & fishery products: Hygiene: Food safety 182
Sheriff Court, Scotland: Act of Sederunt: Shorthand writers: Fees 194
Shetland Islands: Seals: Conservation 194
Ships: Large: Fire protection: Merchant shipping 185
Ships: Small: Fire protection: Merchant shipping 185
Ships: Trans-shipped fish: Ships receiving: Compulsory insurance: Merchant shipping 57
Shore employments: War: Injuries: Compensation 108
Shorthand writers: Fees: Court of Session: Rules: Act of Sederunt 180
Shropshire Cable & Telecoms Ltd.: Public telecommunication systems 22
Shropshire County Council: District of the Wrekin: Local government: Staff transfer 110
Shropshire's Community & Mental Health Services: National Health Service Trust 115
Shropshire's Community Health Service: National Health Service Trust 115
Shropshire's Mental Health: National Health Service Trust 115
Shropshire: Coroners 52
Sierra Leone: Export of goods: United Nations sanctions 3
Singapore: Double taxation relief 5
Skylight Holdings Inc.: Public telecommunication systems 68

Pages 1-23 Jan, 51-69 Feb, 103-131 Mar, 179-196 April

Slovenia: Europe agreement: Association: Definition of treaties: European Communities 181
Smoke control areas: Exempted fireplaces 2
Social fund: Winter fuel payment 22
Social security 128
Social security: Benefits: Up-rating 128, 130
Social security: Child support 4, 21
Social security: Contributions 128
Social security: Contributions & industrial injuries: Canada 67
Social security: Contributions: Re-rating 128
Social security: Contributions: Re-rating & National Insurance Fund payments 128
Social security: Council tax benefit: General 194
Social security: Housing benefit: Permitted totals 127
Social security: Incapacity for work 128
Social security: Income-related benefits: Subsidy to authorities 127
Social security: Industrial injuries: Dependency: Permitted earnings limits 128
Social security: Jobseeker's allowance 21
Social security: Lone parents 127
Social security: Miscellaneous amendments 128
Social security: National Health Service: Pilot schemes 103, 114, 117, 127, 130
Social security: New deal: Miscellaneous provisions 67
Social security: Pensions: Money purchase contracted-out schemes: Reduced rates & rebates 187
Social security: Personal pension schemes: Minimum contributions 187
Social security: Social fund: Winter fuel payment 22
Social security: Statutory maternity pay: Employers: Compensation 128, 130
Social security: Workmen's compensation: Supplementation 128
Social services: Residential care homes: Nursing homes & mental nursing homes 187, 195
Sole: Prohibition of fishing: Specified sea areas 67
Sonic Telecommunications International Ltd.: Public telecommunication systems 129
South & East Wales Ambulance: National Health Service Trust 115
South Atlantic territories: Falkland Islands: Constitution 22
South Cumbria Community & Mental Health: National Health Service Trust 115
South Durham Health Care: National Health Service Trust 115
South Durham: National Health Service Trust 115
South Kent Community Healthcare: National Health Service Trust 116
South Warwickshire Combined Care: National Health Service Trust 116
South Warwickshire Health Care: National Health Service Trust 112
South Warwickshire Mental Health: National Health Service Trust 112
Southern Derbyshire Acute Hospitals: National Health Service Trust 115
Sovereign base areas: Oil pollution: Merchant shipping 184
Specified risk material: Animals 51
Specified risk material: Food 55
Sport, sport competitions & physical education: Value added tax 195
Spreadable fats: Marketing standards 107
St Mark's & Northwick Park: National Health Service Trust 115
St. James & Seacroft University Hospitals: National Health Service Trust 116
St. Peter's Hospital: National Health Service: Trust 112
Staffordshire: Youth court panels 69
Statutory maternity pay: Employers: Compensation 128, 130
Stonehouse & Hairmyres Hospitals: National Hhealth Service Trust 185
Street works: Inspection fees 182
Student loans: Education 54
Student loans: Education: Northern Ireland 58
Suckler cow: Premium quotas 1
Sugar beet: Research & education 129
Sunderland & Tyne Riverside Enterprise zones 106
Superannuation Act 1972: Admission 118
Superannuation: Teachers: Scotland 181
Surface waters: Dangerous substances: Classification 131
Surface waters: Dangerous substances: Classification: Scotland 69

Pages 1-23 Jan, 51-69 Feb, 103-131 Mar, 179-196 April

Surrey & Sussex Healthcare: National Health Service Trust 116
Surrey Hampshire Borders: National Health Service Trust 116
Surrey Heartlands: National Health Service Trust 112
Surrey Oaklands: National Health Service Trust 116
Surrey: East Surrey Healthcare: National Health Service Trust 112
Surrey: East Surrey Priority Care: National Health Service Trust 112
Sussex Cable & Telecoms Ltd.: Public telecommunication systems 22
Sussex: Surrey & Sussex Healthcare: National Health Service Trust 116

T

Taxes: Capital gains tax: Annual exempt amount 129
Taxes: Double taxation relief 5
Taxes: Finance Act 1989: Section 178 (1): Appointed day 108, 129
Taxes: Income tax: Indexation 129
Taxes: Income tax: Retirement benefits schemes: Discretion to approve: Restriction 108
Taxes: Income tax: Retirement benefits schemes: Earnings cap: Indexation 108
Taxes: Inheritance tax: Indexation 108
Taxes: Interest rate 108, 129
Taxes: Value added tax 130
Taxes: Value added tax: Cars 130
Taxes: Value added tax: Fuel: Consideration increase 130
Taxes: Value added tax: Registration limits: Increase 130
Taxes: Value added tax: Special provisions 131
Taxes: Value added tax: Supply of services 131, 195
Teacher training: Funding 54
Teachers' pensions 4
Teachers: Premature retirement & redundancy: Compensation: Scotland 181
Teachers: Schools. Pay & conditions 181
Teachers: Superannuation: Scotland 181
Teeside Development Corporation: Transfer of functions 130
Telecom Ireland Ltd.: Public telecommunication systems 129
Telecommunications: Interconnection 22
Telecommunications: Licensing 22
Telecommunications: Open network provision & leased lines 22
Telecommunications: Public systems: Atlantic Telecommunications Ltd. 129
Telecommunications: Public systems: AXS Telecom (UK) Ltd. 67
Telecommunications: Public systems: Easynet Group Plc 129
Telecommunications: Public systems: Esprit Telecom UK Ltd. 129
Telecommunications: Public systems: Eurobell (Holdings) Plc. 67
Telecommunications: Public systems: Frontel Communications Ltd. 67
Telecommunications: Public systems: GT UK Ltd. 67
Telecommunications: Public systems: HighwayOne Corporation Ltd. 68
Telecommunications: Public systems: IDT Global Ltd. 68
Telecommunications: Public systems: Internet Network Services Ltd. 68
Telecommunications: Public systems: Izencom Ltd. 68
Telecommunications: Public systems: KDD Europe Ltd. 68
Telecommunications: Public systems: LCI Telecom UK Ltd. 129
Telecommunications: Public systems: North American Gateway Ltd. 129
Telecommunications: Public systems: Primetec (UK) Ltd. 129
Telecommunications: Public systems: Shropshire Cable & Telecoms Ltd. 22
Telecommunications: Public systems: Skylight Holdings Inc. 68
Telecommunications: Public systems: Sonic Telecommunications International Ltd. 129
Telecommunications: Public systems: Sussex Cable & Telecoms Ltd. 22
Telecommunications: Public systems: Telecom Ireland Ltd. 129
Telecommunications: Public systems: Telegroup UK Ltd. 129
Telecommunications: Public systems: Teleport (Northern Ireland) Ltd. 68
Telecommunications: Public systems: TGC UK Ltd. 129
Telecommunications: Public systems: The Phone Company 68

Pages 1-23 Jan, 51-69 Feb, 103-131 Mar, 179-196 April

Telegraphs: Videosenders: Interference 195
Telegraphs: Wireless telegraphy: Apparatus: Approval & examination: Fees 22
Telegraphs: Wireless telegraphy: Licence charges 129
Telegraphs: Wireless telegraphy: Television licence: Fees 129
Telegroup UK Ltd.: Public telecommunication systems 129
Teleport (Northern Ireland) Ltd.: Public telecommunication systems 68
Television licence: Fees 129
Terms & conditions of employment 195
Terms & conditions of employment: Disciplinary practice & procedures: Code of practice 22
Terms & conditions of employment: Disclosure of information: Code of practice 22
Terms & conditions of employment: Merchant shipping & fishing vessels 195
Terms & conditions of employment: National Health Service: Pilot schemes 103, 114, 117, 127, 130
Terms & conditions of employment: Social security: Benefits: Up-rating 128, 130
Terms & conditions of employment: Statutory maternity pay: Employers: Compensation 128, 130
Terms & conditions of employment: Time off: Code of practice 22
TGC UK Ltd.: Public telecommunication systems 129
Thames Gateway: National Health Service Trust 116
Thameslink Healthcare: National Health Service Trust 112
Time off: Employment protection: Code of practice 22
Town & country planning: General 22
Town & country planning: General permitted development 130
Town & country planning: General permitted development: Scotland 22
Town & country planning: Urban development corporations: Planning functions: England 22, 23
Town & country planning: Use classes: Scotland 23
Trade marks: Rules 195
Trade: Restrictive practices: Non-notifiable agreements: Sale & purchase, share subscription & franchise agreements 9
Trade: Restrictive practices: Non-notifiable agreements: Turnover threshold 9
Traffic signs: Temporary obstructions 10
Traffic signs: Temporary: Prescribed bodies: England & Wales 10
Traffic: London control system: Transfer 110
Transport & Works Act 1992: Commencement 68
Trial of the Pyx 52
Trunk roads: A1: Abbotsview junction to Oaktree junction 60
Trunk roads: A1: Alnwick 11
Trunk roads: A1: Biggleswade Bypass 121
Trunk roads: A1: C107 Woolley Rd., Cambridgeshire 11
Trunk roads: A1: Carlton on Trent to North Muskham, Nottinghamshire 189
Trunk roads: A1: Clapham Lodge, Londonderry 60
Trunk roads: A1: Dishforth interchange, northbound entry slip road 61
Trunk roads: A1: Elkesley, Bassetlaw, Nottinghamshire 60
Trunk roads: A1: Fairburn to Brotherton 189
Trunk roads: A1: Felton 60
Trunk roads: A1: Fenwick 60
Trunk roads: A1: Ferrybridge interchange 11
Trunk roads: A1: Fiveways Corner, Barnet 121
Trunk roads: A1: Great Ponton, Lincolnshire 61
Trunk roads: A1: Haringey: Red route 9
Trunk roads: A1: Hook Moor interchange 121
Trunk roads: A1: Islington: Red route: Experimental 59
Trunk roads: A1: Junction 38, Redhouse 61
Trunk roads: A1: Lees Lane - Buckden roundabout, Cambridgeshire 11
Trunk roads: A1: Long Bennington, Lincolnshire 61
Trunk roads: A1: Markham Moor roundabout, Nottinghamshire 11
Trunk roads: A1: Micklefield to Bramham 60
Trunk roads: A1: Nene Valley Railway to Water Newton, Cambridgeshire 189
Trunk roads: A1: Norman Cross interchange 11
Trunk roads: A1: North of A63 121
Trunk roads: A1: North of Black Cat to Wyboston 189

Trunk roads: A1: Rainton crossroads	121, 189
Trunk roads: A1: Sandy to Beeston, Bedfordshire	11
Trunk roads: A1: Seaton Burn bypass	61
Trunk roads: A1: Tinwell & Carpenter's Lodge roundabout, nr Stamford	61
Trunk roads: A1: Upper St. & Islington High St., Islington	189
Trunk roads: A1: Wentbridge to Barnsdale Bar	189
Trunk roads: A1: West of Bowerhouse junction to west of Spott junction dualling	59
Trunk roads: A2: Dunkirk	11
Trunk roads: A2: Gravesend east	17
Trunk roads: A2: Lydden to Whitfield	11
Trunk roads: A3: B2070, Buriton	121
Trunk roads: A3: B366, Redhill Rd.	121
Trunk roads: A3: Compton	11
Trunk roads: A3: Farnham Rd.bridge	61
Trunk roads: A3: Guildford & Godalming bypass	121
Trunk roads: A3: Kingston & Wandsworth	59
Trunk roads: A3: Kingston bypass, Kingston upon Thames & Merton	11
Trunk roads: A3: Longmoor interchange	60
Trunk roads: A3: Sheet link, slip roads	121
Trunk roads: A3: West Hill, Wandsworth	11
Trunk roads: A3: Wisley interchange	189
Trunk roads: A4: Bath Rd. & Hatch Lane, Hillingdon	120
Trunk roads: A4: Bath Rd. & Newport Rd., Hillingdon	120
Trunk roads: A4: Bath Road, Hillingdon	121
Trunk roads: A4: Bath Road, Hounslow	121
Trunk roads: A4: Colnbrook bypass, Hillingdon	120
Trunk roads: A4: Colnbrook bypass, Tarmac Way & Stanwell Moor Rd., Hillingdon	120
Trunk roads: A4: Concorde roundabout, Hillingdon	61
Trunk roads: A4: Great West Rd., Hounslow	61
Trunk roads: A4: Keynsham bypass	121
Trunk roads: A5: Cefni Bridge, Anglesey	189
Trunk roads: A5: Churchbridge improvement	55
Trunk roads: A5: Churchbridge improvement: Detrunking	55
Trunk roads: A5: Cornhill to C54 junction, Northamptonshire	189
Trunk roads: A5: Crick, Northamptonshire	11
Trunk roads: A5: Flats Lane to Weeford, Staffordshire	11
Trunk roads: A5: Nr.Lilbourne, Warwickshire	122
Trunk roads: A5: Southeast of Llys-Gwynedd interchange, near Llandegai, Gwynedd	11
Trunk roads: A5: Wall Island improvement	55
Trunk roads: A5: Watling St., Atherstone, Warwickshire	122
Trunk roads: A5: Watling St., Pattishall, Northamptonshire	188
Trunk roads: A5: Watling St., Warwickshire	12
Trunk roads: A6: Buxton Rd., High Lane	12
Trunk roads: A6: Great Glen	122
Trunk roads: A6: Great Glen to Burton Overy, Leicestershire	189
Trunk roads: A6: Great Glen, Leicestershire	122
Trunk roads: A6: Loughborough town centre	61
Trunk roads: A8: East Hamilton St./Sinclair St.junction, Greenock	189
Trunk roads: A8: Greenock Rd., Port Glasgow & Port Glasgow Rd., Greenock	61
Trunk roads: A8: Newark roundabout to Woodhall roundabout	12
Trunk roads: A8: Sinclair St.	122
Trunk roads: A8: Woodhall roundabout to West Ferry interchange	122
Trunk roads: A9: B8033, Queen Victoria School junction	61
Trunk roads: A10: Foxton level crossing, Cambridgeshire	122
Trunk roads: A10: Great Cambridge Road, Enfield	122
Trunk roads: A10: Haringey: Red route	9
Trunk roads: A10: Hilgay to Setchey, Norfolk	122
Trunk roads: A10: Kingsmead viaduct, Ware	122

Pages 1-23 Jan, 51-69 Feb, 103-131 Mar, 179-196 April

232 ALPHABETICAL INDEX

Trunk roads: A12/A127: Gallows Corner flyover, Havering 122
Trunk roads: A12: Brentwood bypass, Essex 61
Trunk roads: A12: Chelmsford bypass 122
Trunk roads: A12: Chelmsford, Essex 61
Trunk roads: A12: Crown interchange, Essex 61
Trunk roads: A12: Eastern Avenue, Redbridge 122
Trunk roads: A12: Feering to Marks Fey, Essex 122
Trunk roads: A12: Hatfield Peverel bypass 122
Trunk roads: A12: Latymere Dam Bridge, Suffolk 12
Trunk roads: A12: Lowestoft to Gorleston 122
Trunk roads: A12: Redbridge: Red route 9
Trunk roads: A12: Stratford St Mary bypass, Essex & Suffolk 12
Trunk roads: A13: Beckton, Canning Town & Barking Rd. flyovers, Newham 12
Trunk roads: A13: Canning Town flyover, Newham 12
Trunk roads: A13: Newham Way, Newham 12
Trunk roads: A14: Bar Hill interchange to Spittals interchange, Huntingdon 122
Trunk roads: A14: Burton Latimer bypass, Northamptonshire 61
Trunk roads: A14: Cambridgeshire & Suffolk 61
Trunk roads: A14: Cambridgeshire to Felixstowe 189
Trunk roads: A14: Huntingdon Rail Viaduct 122
Trunk roads: A14: Lolworth, Cambridgeshire 12
Trunk roads: A16: Spilsby Rd./Dalby Rd., Partney, Lincolnshire 10
Trunk roads: A16: Stickford, Lincs. 122
Trunk roads: A16: Tallington, Lincolnshire 61
Trunk roads: A17: Beckingham bypass, Lincolnshire 62
Trunk roads: A17: Washway Rd., Lincolnshire 12
Trunk roads: A19: Barlby Rd., Selby 123
Trunk roads: A19: Cold Hesledon northbound exit slip road 62
Trunk roads: A19: Fulford - Crockley Hill 12
Trunk roads: A19: Hylton Bridge 123
Trunk roads: A19: Low Leven - Leven viaduct 62
Trunk roads: A19: Parkway junction to Norton interchange 62
Trunk roads: A19: Percy Main Interchange 123
Trunk roads: A19: Skelton - Thirsk 12
Trunk roads: A19: Tollerton 123
Trunk roads: A19: Tyne Tunnel approach road, Jarrow 62
Trunk roads: A20: Marker post 16.60 - 20.60 189
Trunk roads: A20: Round Hill Tunnel 66
Trunk roads: A21: John's Cross 60
Trunk roads: A23: Brighton Rd., Coulsdon 12, 123
Trunk roads: A23: Brighton Rd., Croydon 12
Trunk roads: A23: Croydon: Red route: Prohibited turns 9
Trunk roads: A23: Lambeth: Red route: Experimental 9
Trunk roads: A23: Lambeth: Red route: Prohibition of traffic 59
Trunk roads: A23: London Rd., Croydon 123
Trunk roads: A23: Purley Way, Croydon 123
Trunk roads: A27: Beddingham level crossing 12, 123
Trunk roads: A27: Bognor Road roundabout 123
Trunk roads: A27: Eastern Rd.& Broadmarsh interchanges 62
Trunk roads: A27: Junction 12, Portsbridge 19
Trunk roads: A27: Ranscombe Hill, East Sussex 123
Trunk roads: A27: Ranscombe Lane 62
Trunk roads: A27: Warblington 123
Trunk roads: A30: Alphington interchange 123
Trunk roads: A30: Camborne bypass 189
Trunk roads: A30: Cannaframe Bridge 12
Trunk roads: A30: Fairmile to Hand & Pen 62
Trunk roads: A30: Hawkstor to Colliford 189
Trunk roads: A30: Iron Bridge to Turks Head 12

Pages 1-23 Jan, 51-69 Feb, 103-131 Mar, 179-196 April

ALPHABETICAL INDEX

Trunk roads: A30: Kennards House Junction 123
Trunk roads: A30: Launceston bypass 12
Trunk roads: A30: Mount Pleasant to Innis Downs 189
Trunk roads: A30: Plusha to Bolventor 13
Trunk roads: A30: Tregoss Moor Bridge 190
Trunk roads: A31: Azalea roundabout to Boundary Lane roundabout 123
Trunk roads: A31: Verwood Rd. interchange 13
Trunk roads: A31: West of Wimborne Minster 13
Trunk roads: A34, A38 & A500: Staffordshire bridges 18
Trunk roads: A34: Chilton to Beedon 62
Trunk roads: A34: Churchbridge 55
Trunk roads: A34: Churchbridge: Detrunking 55
Trunk roads: A34: Curridge Rd./Oxford Rd. junction 13
Trunk roads: A34: Harwell to Beedon 13
Trunk roads: A34: Hinksey Hill roundabout to Botley interchange 13
Trunk roads: A34: Kings Worthy - Three Maids Hill 190
Trunk roads: A34: M3, junction 9 13
Trunk roads: A34: Marker post 85.1 - 86.7 123
Trunk roads: A34: Peartree Hill to Hinksey Hill 13
Trunk roads: A34: Whitway to Burghclere 190
Trunk roads: A34: Yarlet, Staffordshire 62
Trunk roads: A36: East Clyffe layby 190
Trunk roads: A36: Shelley Common 20
Trunk roads: A38 64
Trunk roads: A38, A500 & A34: Staffordshire bridges 18
Trunk roads: A38: A61 interchange 62
Trunk roads: A38: Branston to Barton, Staffordshire 124
Trunk roads: A38: Carminow roundabout to White Lodge 13
Trunk roads: A38: Devon Expressway, Chudleigh Station interchange 123
Trunk roads: A38: Devon Expressway, Marsh Mills interchange 123
Trunk roads: A38: Devon Expressway, Peartree interchange 123
Trunk roads: A38: Hereford & Worcester 192
Trunk roads: A38: Ivybridge bypass 62
Trunk roads: A38: Kennford bypass & Splatford interchange 62
Trunk roads: A38: Lantoom layby 124
Trunk roads: A38: South of Naunton, Hereford & Worcester 62
Trunk roads: A39: Allen Valley 62
Trunk roads: A40: Dixton, Monmouthshire 124
Trunk roads: A40: Old Bath Rd., Cheltenham 190
Trunk roads: A40: Sandford Rd., Cheltenham 190
Trunk roads: A40: Western Ave., Ealing & Hammersmith & Fulham 190
Trunk roads: A40: Western Ave., Ealing: Speed limits 120
Trunk roads: A41: Berkhamsted bypass, southbound 62
Trunk roads: A41: Berryfields Junction, Aylesbury 124
Trunk roads: A41: Bourne End, northbound slip roads 13
Trunk roads: A41: Camden 124, 188
Trunk roads: A41: Camden: Red route: Bus lanes 120
Trunk roads: A41: Camden: Temporary prohibition of traffic 9
Trunk roads: A41: Fiveways Corner, Barnet 121
Trunk roads: A41: Gloucester Place/Park Rd., City of Westminster 13
Trunk roads: A41: Tong, Shropshire 62
Trunk roads: A41: Westminster: Red route 59, 188
Trunk roads: A41: Whitchurch Rd., Great Broughton, Chester 62
Trunk roads: A43: Evenley crossroads, Northamptonshire 13, 124
Trunk roads: A43: Weldon, Northamptonshire 13
Trunk roads: A45: Dunchurch highway, Coventry, West Midlands 62
Trunk roads: A45: Fletchamstead highway & Kenpas highway, Coventry 62
Trunk roads: A45: Meridan bypass, Solihull 63
Trunk roads: A45: Nene Valley Way: Widening 182

Pages 1-23 Jan, 51-69 Feb, 103-131 Mar, 179-196 April

234 *ALPHABETICAL INDEX*

Trunk roads: A45: Ryton to Tollbar End, Warwickshire 124
Trunk roads: A46 & A606: Stanton on the Wolds and Widmerpool, Notts 124
Trunk roads: A46: Grafton to Ashton-under-Hill 190
Trunk roads: A46: Hinton crossroads, Wychavon, Hereford & Worcester 13
Trunk roads: A46: Kenilworth bypass, Warwickshire 63
Trunk roads: A46: Lincoln bypass 190
Trunk roads: A46: Norton Lenchwick bypass, Hereford & Worcester 60
Trunk roads: A46: Ratcliffe on the Wreake to Six Hills, Leicestershire 190
Trunk roads: A46: Slip roads, Leicestershire 190
Trunk roads: A46: Stratford northern bypass 13
Trunk roads: A46: Stratford Rd., Nr.Alcester, Warwickshire 124
Trunk roads: A46: Swainswick support works 124, 190
Trunk roads: A47: Church Rd junction, Great Plumstead, Norfolk 190
Trunk roads: A47: East Dereham bypass, Norfolk 190
Trunk roads: A47: Soke Parkway, Peterborough 190
Trunk roads: A47: Uppingham Rd., Bushby, Leicestershire 60
Trunk roads: A47: Wisbech level crossing, Cambridgeshire 13
Trunk roads: A49: Portway, Hereford & Worcester 190
Trunk roads: A50: Blythe Bridge to Queensway, Staffordshire 13
Trunk roads: A50: Derby southern bypass 124
Trunk roads: A50: Doveridge bypass, Derbyshire 63
Trunk roads: A52: Radcliffe-on-Trent, Nottinghamshire 190
Trunk roads: A55: Bryngwran to Holyhead 5
Trunk roads: A55: St Asaph, Denbighshire 63
Trunk roads: A56: Edenfield bypass, Haslingden 63
Trunk roads: A57: Aston bypass 190
Trunk roads: A57: Aston Way, Aston 124
Trunk roads: A57: Darlton to Dunham on Trent, Notts. 124
Trunk roads: A58: Chain Bar - Westfield Lane 190
Trunk roads: A59: A56 junction improvement 107
Trunk roads: A59: Broughton 13
Trunk roads: A59: Longsight Rd. 63
Trunk roads: A59: Whalley bypass 124
Trunk roads: A61: A38 interchange 62
Trunk roads: A63: Austhorpe 63
Trunk roads: A63: Hemingbrough 191
Trunk roads: A63: Leeds Rd., Selby 63
Trunk roads: A63: Mount Pleasant roundabout 63
Trunk roads: A63: Myton Bridge, Hull 124
Trunk roads: A63: Selby 190
Trunk roads: A63: Selby Rd., Northolmby St. & Bridgegate 13
Trunk roads: A64: Bond Hill Ash slip roads 124
Trunk roads: A64: Bond Hill to Fulford 63
Trunk roads: A64: Bramham 14
Trunk roads: A64: Headley Bar 14
Trunk roads: A64: Micklefield to Bramham 60
Trunk roads: A65: Settle 124
Trunk roads: A66: Cockermouth - Embleton 63
Trunk roads: A66: Embleton 14
Trunk roads: A66: Fox Well 124
Trunk roads: A66: Kemplay roundabout to Skirsgill roundabout 191
Trunk roads: A66: Kirkby Thore 124
Trunk roads: A66: Whinfell 125
Trunk roads: A66: Whinfell, Penrith 124
Trunk roads: A68: Byrness - Catcleugh 14
Trunk roads: A69 126
Trunk roads: A69: Haltwhistle 60
Trunk roads: A74: Central reserve, Greenhillstairs 63
Trunk roads: A74: London-Carlisle-Glasgow-Inverness 63

Pages 1-23 Jan, 51-69 Feb, 103-131 Mar, 179-196 April

ALPHABETICAL INDEX

Trunk roads: A74: Paddy's Rickle Bridge-Harthope Special Rd. 188
Trunk roads: A74: Southbound entry slip road, Floriston 14
Trunk roads: A75: Glen improvement 188
Trunk roads: A75: Springholm 188
Trunk roads: A77: Ballantrae & Kirkoswald, restricted roads 10
Trunk roads: A77: Fenwick & Raithburn 63
Trunk roads: A77: Girvan Station Bridge 14
Trunk roads: A77: Lendalfoot 60
Trunk roads: A77: Whitletts roundabout improvement 59
Trunk roads: A78: Greenock 14
Trunk roads: A78: High St. & Inverkip St., Greenock 191
Trunk roads: A78: Inverkip Rd., Greenock 63, 125
Trunk roads: A78: Inverkip St., Greenock 191
Trunk roads: A78: Largs 14
Trunk roads: A80: Moodiesburn 125
Trunk roads: A80: Northbound off/on slip roads at Mollinsburn junction 14
Trunk roads: A80: Old Inns interchange south east slip roads 125
Trunk roads: A82: Strowanswell Rd.junction, Dumbarton 191
Trunk roads: A86: Rubha Na Magach to Aberarder 188
Trunk roads: A90: Bridge of Dee 63
Trunk roads: A90: Eastbound between Forfar Rd.& Old Glamis Rd., Dundee 14
Trunk roads: A90: North Anderson Drive 125
Trunk roads: A92: B969, Glenrothes 14
Trunk roads: A96: Blackburn to Kintore bypass 14
Trunk roads: A96: Inveramsay Bridge 14
Trunk roads: A96: Raigmore interchange to West Seafield improvement 14, 60
Trunk roads: A102 and A102(M): Blackwall Tunnel and East Cross Route 125
Trunk roads: A102: Blackwall Tunnel approach roads and southbound tunnel 125
Trunk roads: A102: Blackwall Tunnel northern approach 125
Trunk roads: A102: Blackwall Tunnel northern approach, Tower Hamlets 14
Trunk roads: A102: East Cross route, Hackney 14
Trunk roads: A106: Grove Green Rd., Waltham Forest 14
Trunk roads: A120: Birchanger roundabout 19
Trunk roads: A127/A12: Gallows Corner flyover, Havering 122
Trunk roads: A127: Southend Arterial Rd., Havering 125
Trunk roads: A136: Station Rd., Parkeston 108
Trunk roads: A140: Coddenham, Suffolk 14
Trunk roads: A167: Blind Lane interchange - Picktree Lane roundabout 191
Trunk roads: A167: Burn Hall, Durham 63
Trunk roads: A167: Sacriston Road Bridge, Durham 14
Trunk roads: A174: Marton Interchange 125
Trunk roads: A180: Stallingborough - Great Coates 63
Trunk roads: A205: Brownhill Rd. & Plassy Rd., Catford 16
Trunk roads: A205: Brownhill Rd., Lewisham 16
Trunk roads: A205: Greenwich: Red route 121
Trunk roads: A205: Greenwich: Red route: Banned turns 9
Trunk roads: A205: Greenwich: Red route: Experimental 188
Trunk roads: A205: Lambeth: Red route 188
Trunk roads: A205: Lambeth: Red route: Experimental 121
Trunk roads: A205: Lewisham: Bus lanes: Red route 188
Trunk roads: A205: Lewisham: Red route: Experimental 9
Trunk roads: A205: Southwark: Red route: Bus lanes: Experimental 9
Trunk roads: A205: Southwark: Red route: Experimental 9, 59
Trunk roads: A205: Stansted Rd., Catford 16
Trunk roads: A205: Stansted Rd., Forest Hill 16
Trunk roads: A205: Westhorne Ave., Lewisham 16
Trunk roads: A249: Bluetown, Sheerness 15
Trunk roads: A249: Grovehurst interchange slip roads 15
Trunk roads: A249: Kingsferry Bridge 15, 125

Pages 1-23 Jan, 51-69 Feb, 103-131 Mar, 179-196 April

Trunk roads: A259: High Street, Sandgate, Folkestone ... 125
Trunk roads: A259: Hythe Rd., Dymchurch ... 15
Trunk roads: A303: Andover bypass ... 125
Trunk roads: A303: Andover bypass - A3057 to A343 ... 125
Trunk roads: A303: Bullington Cross ... 15
Trunk roads: A303: Burton junction, Wiltshire ... 63
Trunk roads: A303: Picket Twenty interchange ... 20
Trunk roads: A312: Great West Rd., Hounslow ... 64
Trunk roads: A312: The Parkway, Hounslow ... 15
Trunk roads: A316: Richmond: Red route ... 9
Trunk roads: A339: Headley & Kingsclere ... 191
Trunk roads: A339: Ringway north/east & Kingsclere Rd. ... 15
Trunk roads: A405: Noke roundabout ... 64
Trunk roads: A406: Beckton, Canning Town & Barking Rd. flyovers, Newham ... 12
Trunk roads: A406: Enfield ... 65
Trunk roads: A406: Great Cambridge Rd.underpass, Enfield ... 126
Trunk roads: A406: Hanger Lane & Ashbourne Rd., Ealing ... 59
Trunk roads: A406: Ilford viaduct & Redbridge viaduct, Redbridge ... 16
Trunk roads: A406: Pinkham Way, Barnet ... 65, 191
Trunk roads: A406: South Woodford to Barking Relief Rd., Redbridge ... 16
Trunk roads: A414: London Colney roundabout ... 191
Trunk roads: A414: Whitehorse Lane, London Colney ... 64
Trunk roads: A417: Duntisbourne Abbots ... 15
Trunk roads: A419: Horse & Groom link ... 64
Trunk roads: A419: Latton link ... 64
Trunk roads: A421: Bedfordshire ... 191
Trunk roads: A423: Banbury Rd., Watergall, Warwickshire ... 64
Trunk roads: A423: Coventry Road, Long Itchington ... 125
Trunk roads: A428: Bedfordshire ... 191
Trunk roads: A435: Gorcott Hill, Warwickshire & Hereford & Worcester ... 64
Trunk roads: A446: Lichfield Rd., Curdworth, Warwickshire ... 64
Trunk roads: A449 ... 125
Trunk roads: A449: Acton Gate, Staffordshire ... 64
Trunk roads: A449: Hereford & Worcester & Gloucestershire ... 20
Trunk roads: A453: Clifton Lane, Nottinghamshire ... 125
Trunk roads: A456: Worcester Rd., Hagley, Hereford & Worcester ... 15
Trunk roads: A465: Merthyr Tydfil, Merthyr Tydfil County Borough ... 191
Trunk roads: A470: Abercynon, Rhondda Cynon Taff ... 64
Trunk roads: A470: Ty Nant to north Maentwrog Rd.Station improvement ... 108
Trunk roads: A470: Upper Boat, Rhondda Cynon Taff ... 125
Trunk roads: A483: Ruabon, Wrexham ... 191
Trunk roads: A487: Bus stop lay-bys, north of Caernarfon, Gwynedd ... 15
Trunk roads: A487: Upper Corris, Gwynedd, restricted roads ... 11
Trunk roads: A494: Rhydymain, Gwynedd ... 126
Trunk roads: A500, A34 & A38: Staffordshire bridges ... 18
Trunk roads: A500: Queensway, Newcastle Under Lyme, Staffordshire ... 15
Trunk roads: A501: Camden ... 64
Trunk roads: A501: Camden & Westminster: Red route ... 60
Trunk roads: A501: City Rd., Islington ... 64
Trunk roads: A501: Euston Rd., Camden: Red route: Prescribed routes ... 10
Trunk roads: A516 ... 64
Trunk roads: A523: Ashbourne Rd., Leek, Staffordshire ... 64
Trunk roads: A523: Ashbourne Rd., Staffordshire ... 191
Trunk roads: A523: London Rd., Macclesfield ... 64
Trunk roads: A523: Lowe Hill, Leek, Staffordshire ... 15
Trunk roads: A556 ... 126
Trunk roads: A556: Northwich bypass ... 126
Trunk roads: A557: Widnes eastern bypass, southern section ... 64

Pages 1-23 Jan, 51-69 Feb, 103-131 Mar, 179-196 April

Trunk roads: A570: Rainford bypass 15
Trunk roads: A580: East Lancashire Rd. 15
Trunk roads: A580: East Lancashire Rd., Golborne 191
Trunk roads: A580: Knowsley Wood Lane 15
Trunk roads: A585: Skippool roundabout 64
Trunk roads: A595: Various locations 15
Trunk roads: A596: Flimby 64
Trunk roads: A596: Maryport 15
Trunk roads: A596: Workington Bridge 191
Trunk roads: A614: Old Rufford Rd., near Blidworth, Nottinghamshire 15
Trunk roads: A616/A628: A628 principal road, Flough junction 60, 64
Trunk roads: A628/A616: A628 principal road, Flough junction 60, 64
Trunk roads: A629: Aire Valley Rd., Keighley 15
Trunk roads: A638: Bawtry Rd., Doncaster 191
Trunk roads: A638: Junction of Bawtry Rd.& the B6463 Sheep Bridge Lane 16
Trunk roads: A638: Offley Lane 126
Trunk roads: A646: Holme Chapel Bridge 126
Trunk roads: A650: Saltaire roundabout 64
Trunk roads: A663: Broadway 65
Trunk roads: A666: Kearsley Spur 193
Trunk roads: A725/A726: High Blantyre 191
Trunk roads: A725/A726: Westbound on & off slip roads to & from Glasgow Rd., Blantyre 64
Trunk roads: A725: Bellziehill & Diamond interchanges 16
Trunk roads: A725: Whirlies roundabout to Birniehill roundabout 16
Trunk roads: A726: Eastbound cycletrack between Righead & Murray roundabouts 16
Trunk roads: A737: Dalry 65
Trunk roads: A737: Kilbarchan interchange slips to Elliston junction 65
Trunk roads: A737: Linclive interchange to M8 junction 28A & St James 16
Trunk roads: A876: Kincardine Bridge 16
Trunk roads: A972: Kingsway, Pitkerro Rd.footbridge 65
Trunk roads: A1033: Mount Pleasant roundabout 63
Trunk roads: A1041: Carlton 11
Trunk roads: A1041: Selby 190
Trunk roads: A1079: Dunnington & Kexby 65
Trunk roads: A1079: Hayton 65
Trunk roads: A1307: Girton interchange, Cambridgeshire 126
Trunk roads: A1400: Redbridge: Red route 10
Trunk roads: A4076: Victoria Bridge, Milford Haven improvement 5
Trunk roads: A5103: Princess Parkway 65
Trunk roads: A5148: Wall Island improvement 55
Trunk roads: A5195: Birmingham northern relief road link road 55
Trunk roads: A6120: Leeds Outer Ring Road, Weetwood Lane junction 126
Trunk roads: A6120: Moor Allerton 191
Trunk roads: A6120: Station Rd., Cross Gates 191
Trunk roads: B5404: Mile Oak to Pennine Way, Staffordshire 126
Trunk roads: B776: Westbound on & off slip roads to & from Glasgow Rd., Blantyre 64
Trunk roads: London Borough of Haringey: Red route: Bus lanes 188
Trunk roads: London Borough of Lambeth: Red route: Bus lanes 60
Trunk roads: Route A78: Restricted road, Fairlie 11
Trunk roads: Scotland 21
Trunk roads: Various: Cambridgeshire, Essex, Norfolk & Suffolk 21
Tunbridge Wells Borough Council: Local government: Defined activities: Exemption 110
Tunnels: Tyne Tunnel: Tolls & traffic classification: Revision 182
Tyneside: Cheviot & Wansbeck, North Tyneside Health Care: National Health Service Trust 112

U

United Leeds Teaching Hospitals: National Health Service Trust 116
United Nations sanctions: Dependent territories: Federal Republic of Yugoslavia 195

Pages 1-23 Jan, 51-69 Feb, 103-131 Mar, 179-196 April

238 ALPHABETICAL INDEX

United Nations sanctions: Export of goods: Sierra Leone 3
United Nations sanctions: Federal Republic of Yugoslavia 195
United Reformed Church Acts 1972 & 1981: Jersey 105
University College Hospital: Special trustees: National Health Service Trust 185
Urban development corporations: Area & constitution: England 23, 130
Urban Development Corporations: Dissolution: England 195
Urban development corporations: Planning functions: England 22, 23
Urban development corporations: Property, rights & liabilities: Transfer: Commission for the New Towns: England 23
Urban development: London Docklands Development Corporation 68
Urban development: London Docklands Development Corporation: Functions: Transfer 130
Urban development: London Docklands Development Corporation: Property, etc.: Transfer: Lee Valley Regional Park Authorit 130
Urban development: London Docklands Development Corporation: Property, etc.: Transfer: Urban Regeneration Agency 130
Urban development: London Docklands Development Corporation: Property, rights & liabilities: Transfer . . 23
Urban development: Teesside Development Corporation: Transfer of functions 130
Uzbekistan: Partnership & co-operation agreement: Definition of treaties: European Communities 181

V

Valuation & rating: Exempted classes: Scotland 120
Value added tax 23, 130
Value added tax: Cars 130
Value added tax: Fuel: Consideration increase 130
Value added tax: Place of supply of services 195
Value added tax: Registration limits: Increase 130
Value added tax: Special provisions 131
Value added tax: Sport, sport competitions & physical education 195
Value added tax: Supply of services 131, 195
Vehicle emissions: Fixed penalty 10
Vehicle excise duty: Immobilisation, removal & disposal of vehicles 10
Veterinary drugs: Merchants in: Exemptions 184
Veterinary medicinal products: Administration: Restrictions 7
Veterinary practitioners: Registration 68
Veterinary surgeons: Commonwealth & foreign candidates: Examination 68
Veterinary surgeons: Registration 68
Video recording: Silent: Interviews: Northern Ireland (Emergency Provisions) Act 1996 58
Video recordings: Labelling 131
Videosenders: Interference: Telegraphs 195
Visas: Transit visas: Immigration 182
Visiting forces & international headquarters: Application of law 53
Vocational training: General medical practice: National Health Service 111, 114, 117
Vocational training: General medical practice: National Health Service: Scotland 7

W

Wales: Council tax: Demand notices 104
Wales: Council tax: Prescribed classes of dwellings 53
Wales: Council tax: Reduction scheme: Local government 104
Wales: Environmental protection: Financial assistance 107
Wales: Grant-maintained & grant-maintained special schools: Finance 105
Wales: Mid Glamorgan Ambulance: National Health Service Trust 113
Wales: National Health Service: Originating capital debt 114
Wales: Non-domestic rating: Contributions 8
Wales: Non-domestic rating: Demand notices: Rural rate relief 59
Wales: Non-domestic rating: Rural settlements: Local government 8, 120
Wales: North Wales Ambulance: National Health Service Trust 115
Wales: North: Combined probation areas 8

Pages 1-23 Jan, 51-69 Feb, 103-131 Mar, 179-196 April

Wales: Rating & valuation: Non-domestic rating: Rural settlements ... 8, 120
Wales: South & East Wales Ambulance: National Health Service Trust ... 115
Wales: West Wales Ambulance: National Health Service Trust ... 116
Walsgrave Hospitals: National Health Service Trust ... 116
Wandsworth London Borough: Special parking areas ... 121
Wansbeck & Cheviot, North Tyneside Health Care: National Health Service Trust ... 112
War: Injuries: Compensation: Shore employments ... 108
Warwickshire: North Warwickshire: National Health Service Trust ... 115
Warwickshire: South Warwickshire Health Care: National Health Service Trust ... 112
Warwickshire: South Warwickshire Mental Health: National Health Service Trust ... 112
Waste management: Licensing ... 107
Waste recycling payments: Environmental protection ... 106
Waste: Controlled: Carriers: Registration: Seizure of vehicles ... 106
Water industry: Chester Waterworks Company: Constitution & regulation ... 68
Water pollution: Prevention: Loch Turret, Scotland ... 68
Water resources: England & Wales ... 195
Water resources: England & Wales: Mines: Notice of abandonment ... 196
Water resources: Surface waters: Dangerous substances: Classification ... 131
Water services: Charges: Billing & collection: Scotland ... 131
Water supply: Sewerage: Domestic charges: Reduction: Scotland ... 131
Water supply: Water services: Charges: Billing & collection: Scotland ... 131
Water: Surface waters: Dangerous substances: Classification: Scotland ... 69
Weights & measures: Non-automatic weighing instruments ... 23
Welfare: Food ... 107
Welsh Ambulance Services: National Health Service Trust ... 116
West Wales Ambulance: National Health Service Trust ... 116
Westminster & Roehampton Hospitals: Special trustees: National Health Service Trust ... 116
Westmorland Hospitals: National Health Service Trust ... 116
Wheeled child conveyances: Safety ... 2
Wildlife & Countryside Act 1981: Variation ... 131
Wildlife: Conservation: Natural habitats, &c. ... 2, 23
Wine: Common agricultural policy ... 103
Winter fuel payment: Social fund ... 22
Wireless telegraphy: Apparatus: Approval & examination: Fees ... 22
Wireless telegraphy: Licence charges ... 129
Wireless telegraphy: Television licence: Fees ... 129
Wireless telegraphy: Videosenders: Interference ... 195
Worcester & Hereford: Coroners ... 52
Work: Incapacity: Social security ... 128
Workmen's compensation: Supplementation ... 128

Y

Yorkshire South constituency: European Parliamentary elections: Day of by-election ... 120
Youth courts & offenders: Devon ... 69
Youth courts & offenders: Gwent ... 69
Youth courts & offenders: Hampshire ... 69
Youth courts & offenders: Staffordshire ... 69
Yugoslavia, Federal Republic of: Dependent territories: United Nations sanctions ... 195
Yugoslavia: Federal Republic of: United Nations sanctions ... 195

**List of
Statutory Rules
of
Northern Ireland**

Preface

The *List* contains:

(a) a list of the Northern Ireland statutory rules which appeared in the *Daily list* during the month, arranged under their subject headings. The information given includes the enabling power, as set out in italics, and the date when the rules were issued, made and laid and comes into force so far as applicable to each rule; paginations; ISBN and price;

(b) a numerical list of the same statutory rules, with their subject headings;

(c a list of commencement orders;

(d) an alphabetical subject index.

Details of statutory rules from 1983 may be found in the monthly and annual *List of statutory instruments together with the list of statutory rules for Northern Ireland ...*

The full text of statutory rules may be found in the annual volumes of statutory rules which are issued in two parts.

Please note that statutory rules of Northern Ireland are only available from the Stationery Office's Belfast Bookshop (address on back cover).

LIST OF STATUTORY RULES OF NORTHERN IRELAND BY SUBJECT HEADING

AGRICULTURE

Feeding Stuffs (Amendment) Regulations (Northern Ireland) 1998. No. 124. – Enabling power:Agriculture Act 1970, ss. 66 (1), 68 (1), 69 (1) (3) (6) (7), 74A, 84, 86. Issued:31.03.1998. Made:25.03.1998. Coming into force: 04.05.1998. Effect: S.R. 1995/451 amended. – 28p. – 0 337 93106 2 *£4.70*

CRIMINAL PROCEDURE

The Proceeds of Crime (Countries and Territories designated under the Criminal Justice Act 1988) Order (Northern Ireland) 1998. No. 88. – Enabling power:S.I. 1996/1299 (N.I. 9), art. 42. Issued: 31.03.1998. Made:10.03.1998. Coming into force:27.04.1998. Effect:S.R. 1992/198 revoked. – 48p. – 0 337 93084 8 *£6.45*

DANGEROUS DRUGS

Misuse of Drugs (Amendment) Regulations (Northern Ireland) 1998. No. 128. – Enabling power:Misuse of Drugs Act 1971, ss. 7, 10, 31. – Issued:07.04.1998. Made:31.03.1998. Coming into force:01.05.1998. Effect:S.R. 1986/52 amended. – 4p. – 0 337 93111 9 *£1.10*

EDUCATION

Curriculum (Programme of Study and Attainment Targets in Irish in Irish Speaking Schools at Key Stages 3 and 4) Order (Northern Ireland) 1998. No. 118. – Enabling power:S.I. 1989/2406 (NI. 20) art. 7 (1) (a) (5). – Issued:07.04.1998. Made:19.03.1998. Coming into force:01.08.1998, 01.08.1999., 01.08.2000. In acc. with arts. 2 & 3. Effect:None. – 4p. – 0 337 93105 4 *£1.10*

The Education Reform (1989 Order) (Commencement No. 9) Order (Northern Ireland) 1998. No. 119 (C. 5). – Enabling power:S.I. 1989/2406 (NI. 20) art. 1 (3) (4). Bringing into operation various provisions of the 1989 Order on 19.03.1998., 31.07.1998. & 31.07.1999. – Issued:07.04.1998. Made:19.03.1998. Effect:None. – 8p. – 0 337 93107 0 *£1.95*

Education Reform (Amendment) Order (Northern Ireland) 1998. No. 117. – Enabling power:S.I. 1989/2406 (NI. 20), art. 6 (6). – Issued:09.04.1998. Made:19.03.1998. Coming into force:30.07.1998. Effect:S.I. 1989/2406 (NI. 20) amended. – 2p. – 0 337 93103 8 *£0.65*

School Admissions (Appeal Tribunals) Regulations (Northern Ireland) 1998. No. 115. – Enabling power:S.I. 1997/866 (NI.5), art. 15 (8) & S.I. 1986/594 (NI.3), art. 134 (1). – Issued:25.03.1998. Made:18.03.1998. Coming into operation:01.04.1998. Effect:S.R. 1990/126; 1991/218; 1994/238 revoked with savings. – 8p. – 0 337 93087 2 *£1.55*

EMPLOYMENT AND TRAINING

New Deal (Miscellaneous Provisions) Order (Northern Ireland) 1998. No. 127. – Enabling power:S.I. 1988/1087 (NI. 10), art.4. – Issued:07.04.1998. Made:31.03.1998. Coming into force:11.05.1998. Effect:None. – 6p. – 0 337 93113 5 *£1.55*

HARBOURS, DOCKS, ETC.

The Ports (Levy on Disposals of Land, etc.) (Amendment) Order (Northern Ireland) 1998. No. 148. – Enabling power:S.I. 1994/2809 (N.I. 16), art. 19.. – Issued:16.04.1998. Made:07.04.1998. Coming into force:19.05.1998. Effect:S.R. 1997/12 amended. – 2p. – 0 337 93121 6 *£0.65*

HEALTH AND PERSONAL SOCIAL SERVICES

Charges for Drugs and Appliances (Amendment) Regulations (Northern Ireland) 1998. No. 94. – Enabling power:S.I. 1972/1265 (NI.14), arts. 98, 106, sch. 15. – Issued:25.03.1998. Made:11.03.1998. Coming into operation:01.04.1998. Effect:S.I. 1997/382 amended. – 4p. – 0 337 93085 6 *£1.10*

The Health and Personal Social Services (Assessment of Resources) (Amendment) Regulations (Northern Ireland) 1998. No. 138. – Enabling power:S.I. 1972/1265 (NI. 14), arts. 36 (6), 99 (5) (d). – Issued:10.04.1998. Made:25.03.1998. Coming into force:01.04.1998. Effect:S.R. 1993/127 amended. – 0 337 93124 0 *£1.10*

The North Down and Ards Community Health and Social Services Trust (Dissolution) Order (Northern Ireland) 1998. No. 123. – 2p. – Enabling power:S.I. 1991/194 (N.I. 1), paras. 23 (1), sch. 3. – Issued:16.04.1998. Made:25.03.1998. Coming into force:01.04.1998. Effect:S.R. 1993/354 revoked. – 4p. – 0 337 93125 9 *£0.65*

Pharmaceutical Services (Amendment) Regulations (Northern Ireland) 1998. No. 95. – Enabling power:S.I. 1972/1265 (NI.14), arts. 63 (1) (2), 106 (b), 107 (6). – Issued:25.03.1998. Made:11.03.1998. Coming into operation:01.05.1998. Effect:S.I. 1997/381 amended. – 2p. – 0 337 93083 X *£0.65*

The Ulster Community and Hospitals Health and Social Services Trust (Establishment) Order (Northern Ireland) 1998. No. 121. – Enabling power:S.I. 1991/194 (NI. 1), art. 10 (1), sch. 3, paras. 1, 3, 3A, 4, 5, 6 (2) (d). – Issued:10.04.1998. Made:25.03.1998. Coming into force:01.04.1998. Effect:None. – 4p. – 0 337 93122 4 *£1.10*

Price/availability liable to change without notice

244 HEALTH AND SAFETY

The Ulster, North Down and Ards Hospitals Health and Social Services Trust (Dissolution) Order (Northern Ireland) 1998. No. 122. – Enabling power:S.I. 1991/194 (N.I. 1), paras. 23 (1), sch. 3.. – Issued:16.04.1998. Made:25.03.1998. Coming into force:01.04.1998. Effect:S.R. 1992/494 revoked. – 2p. – 0 337 93123 2 £0.65

HEALTH AND SAFETY

Health and Safety (Fees) Regulations (Northern Ireland) 1998. No. 125. – Enabling power:S.I. 1978/1039 (N.I. 9), arts. 40(2)(4), 49, 55(2). Issued:31.03.1998. Made:26.03.1998. Coming into force:05.05.1998. Effect: S.R. 1984/205; 1992/2; 1994/6, 143; 1997/225, 249 amended & S.R. 1997/29, 234 revoked. – 20p. – 0 337 93104 6 £3.70

HOUSING

The Housing Benefit (General) (Amendment No. 2) Regulations (Northern Ireland) 1998. No. 114. – Enabling power:Social Security Contributions and Benefits (Northern Ireland) Act 1992, ss. 122 (1) (d), 129 (4). – Issued:25.03.1998. Made:19.03.1998. Coming into operation:01.06.1998. Effect:S.R. 1987/461 amended. – 4p. – 0 337 93086 4 £1.10

The Social Security (Amendment) (Lone Parents) Regulations (Northern Ireland) 1998. No. 112. – Enabling power:Social Security Contributions and Benefits (Northern Ireland) Act 1992, ss. 122 (1) (a) (d), 129 (2) (4), 131 (1), 132 (4) (b), 133 92) (i), 171 (1) (3) (4) & S.I. 1995/2705 (NI.15), arts. 6 (5), 143 (2) (4) (b), 36 (2). – Issued:25.03.1998. Made:18.03.1998. Coming into operation:06.04.1998. Effect:S.R. 1987/459, 461; 1996/198; 1998/59 amended & S.R. 1997/354 revoked. – 12p. – 0 337 93089 9 £2.40

LANDS TRIBUNAL

Lands Tribunal (Salaries) Order (Northern Ireland) 1998. No. 155. – Enabling power:Lands Tribunal and Compensation Act (Northern Ireland) 1964, s. 2 (5) & Administrative and Financial Provisions Act (Northern Ireland) 1962, s. 18. – Issued:22.04.1998. Made:08.04.1998. Coming into force:27.05.1998. Effect:S.R. 1997/296 revoked. – 2p. – 0 337 93118 6 £0.65

LEGAL AID AND ADVICE

Legal Advice and Assistance (Amendment) Regulations (Northern Ireland) 1998. No. 90. – Enabling power:S.I. 1981/228 (N.I. 8), arts. 7 (2), 14, 22, 27. Issued: 31.03.1998. Made: 04.03.1998. Coming in to force: 06.04.1998. Effect:S.R. 1981/366 amended & S.R. 1997/91 revoked. – 4p. – 0 337 93082 1 £1.10

Legal Aid (Assessment of Resources) (Amendment) Regulations (Northern Ireland) 1998. No. 89. – Enabling power:S.I. 1981/228 (N.I. 8), arts. 14, 22, 27. Issued: 31.03.1998. Made:04.03.1998. Coming into force:06.04.1998. Effect:S.R. 1981/189 amended. – 4p. – 0 337 93112 7 £1.10

LOCAL GOVERNMENT

Local Government (Superannuation) (Amendment) Regulations (Northern Ireland) 1998. No. 133. – Enabling power:S.I. 1972/1073 (NI. 10), art. 9, sch. 3. – Issued:10.04.1998. Made:31.03.1998. Coming into force:25.05.1998. Effect:S.R. 1992/547 amended. – 2p. – 0 337 93126 7 £0.65

MAGISTRATES' COURTS

The Courses for Drink-Drive Offenders (Designation of District) Order (Northern Ireland) 1998. No. 68. – Enabling power:S.I. 1996/1320 (NI.10), art. 39 (4) (6). – Issued:19.03.1998. Made:04.03.1998. Coming into operation:31.03.1998. Effect:None. – 2p. – 0 337 93071 6 £0.65

PENSIONS

The Social Security (Minimum Contributions to Appropriate Personal Pension Schemes) Order (Northern Ireland) 1998. No. 136. – Enabling power:Pension Schemes (Northern Ireland) Act 1993, s. 41A. – Issued:07.04.1998. Made:02.04.1998. Coming into force:06.04.1999. Effect:S.R. 1996/151 amended. – 6p. – 0 337 93102 X £1.55

The Social Security (Reduced Rates of Class 1 Contributions, and Rebates) (Money Purchase Contracted-out Schemes) Order (Northern Ireland) 1998. No. 137. – Enabling power:Pension Schemes (Northern Ireland) Act 1993, s. 38B. – Issued:07.04.1998. Made:02.04.1998. Coming into force:06.04.1999. Effect:S.R. 1996/150 amended. – 6p. – 0 337 93101 1 £1.55

PLANNING

Planning (Control of Advertisements) (Amendment) Regulations (Northern Ireland) 1998. No. 147. – Enabling power:S.I. 1991/1220 (NI. 11), art. 67 (1) (2). – Issued:10.04.1998. Made:06.04.1998. Coming into force:18.05.1998. Effect:S.R. 1992/448 amended. – 8p. – 0 337 93128 3 £1.95

PLANT HEALTH

The Plant Health (Amendment No. 2) Order (Northern Ireland) 1998. No. 146. – Enabling power:Plant Health Act 1967, ss. 2, 3 (1), 3A, 3B (1), 4 (1). – Issued:10.04.1998. Made:06.04.1998. Coming into force:11.05.1998. Effect:S.R. 1993/256 amended. – 4p. – 0 337 93127 5 £1.10

Price/availability liable to change without notice

RACE RELATIONS
Race Relations (Complaints to Industrial Tribunals) (Armed Forces) Regulations (Northern Ireland) 1998. No. 104. – Enabling power:S.I. 1997/869 (NI.6), art. 71 (9). – Issued:02.04.1998. Made:28.02.1998. Coming into operation:17.04.1998. Effect:None. – 2p. – 0 337 93093 7 £0.65

RATES
The Social Security (Amendment) (Lone Parents) Regulations (Northern Ireland) 1998. No. 112. – Enabling power:Social Security Contributions and Benefits (Northern Ireland) Act 1992, ss. 122 (1) (a) (d), 129 (2) (4), 131 (1), 132 (4) (b), 133 92) (i), 171 (1) (3) (4) & S.I. 1995/2705 (NI.15), arts. 6 (5), 143 (2) (4) (b), 36 (2). – Issued:25.03.1998. Made:18.03.1998. Coming into operation:06.04.1998. Effect:S.R. 1987/459, 461; 1996/198; 1998/59 amended & S.R. 1997/354 revoked. – 12p. – 0 337 93089 9 £2.40

REGISTERED HOMES
The Nursing Homes (Amendment) Regulations (Northern Ireland) 1998. No. 140. – Enabling power:S.I. 1992/3204 (N.I. 20), arts. 19 (3) (7), 36 (2).. – Issued:16.04.1998. Made:03.04.1998. Coming into force:01.05.1998. Effect:S.R. 1993/92 amended. – 2p. – 0 337 93120 8 £0.65

The Residential Care Homes (Amendment) Regulations (Northern Ireland) 1998. No. 139. – Enabling power:S.I. 1992/3204 (N.I. 20), arts. 6 (3) (8), 36 (2).. – Issued:16.04.1998. Made:03.04.1998. Coming into force:01.05.1998. Effect:S.R. 1993/91 amended. – 2p. – 0 337 93119 4 £0.65

ROAD AND RAILWAY TRANSPORT
Level Crossing (Balnamore) Order (Northern Ireland) 1998. No. 143. – Enabling power:Transport Act (Northern Ireland) 1967, s. 66 (1) (2). – Issued:09.04.1998. Made:03.04.1998. Coming into force:15.05.1998. Effect:S.R. 1982/156; 1989/225 amended & 1975/118 revoked. – 9p. – 0 337 93098 8 £1.95

Level Crossing (Coldagh) Order (Northern Ireland) 1998. No. 144. – Enabling power:Transport Act (Northern Ireland) 1967, s. 66 (1) (2). – Issued:09.04.1998. Made:03.04.1998. Coming into force:15.05.1998. Effect:S.R. 1982/156 amended & 1975/122; 1989/225 revoked. – 8p. – 0 337 93129 1 £1.95

Level Crossing (Damhead North) Order (Northern Ireland) 1998. No. 141. – Enabling power:Transport Act (Northern Ireland) 1967, s. 66 (1) (2). – Issued:10.04.1998. Made:03.04.1998. Coming into force:15.05.1998. Effect:S.R. 1982/156; 1989/225 amended & 1975/121 revoked. – 9p. – 0 337 93099 6 £1.95

Level Crossing (Macfinn) Order (Northern Ireland) 1998. No. 142. – Enabling power:Transport Act (Northern Ireland) 1967, s. 66 (1) (2). – Issued:10.04.1998. Made:03.04.1998. Coming into force:15.05.1998. Effect:S.R. 1982/156; 1989/225 amended & 1975/123 revoked. – 9p. – 0 337 93100 3 £1.95

ROAD TRAFFIC AND VEHICLES
The Courses for Drink-Drive Offenders (Designation of District) Order (Northern Ireland) 1998. No. 68. – Enabling power:S.I. 1996/1320 (NI.10), art. 39 (4) (6). – Issued:19.03.1998. Made:04.03.1998. Coming into operation:31.03.1998. Effect:None. – 2p. – 0 337 93071 6 £0.65

Motor Vehicles (Construction and Use) (Amendment) Regulations (Northern Ireland) 1998. No. 116. Enabling power:S.I. 1995/2994 (N.I. 18), arts. 55 (1) (2) (6), 110 (2). Issued:31.03.1998. Made:20.03.1998. Coming into force:01.05.1998. Effect:S.R. 1989/299 amended. – 4p. – 0 337 93110 0 £1.10

SEX DISCRIMINATION
Sex Discrimination (Complaints to Industrial Tribunals) (Armed Forces) Regulations (Northern Ireland) 1998. No. 106. – Enabling power:S.I. 1976/1042 (NI.15), art. 82 (9C). – Issued:02.04.1998. Made:28.02.1998. Coming into operation:17.04.1998. Effect:None. – 2p. – 0 337 93092 9 £0.65

SOCIAL SECURITY
New Deal (Miscellaneous Provisions) Order (Northern Ireland) 1998. No. 127. – Enabling power:S.I. 1988/1087 (NI. 10), art.4. – Issued:07.04.1998. Made:31.03.1998. Coming into force:11.05.1998. Effect:None. – 6p. – 0 337 93113 5 £1.55

The Social Security (Amendment) (Lone Parents) Regulations (Northern Ireland) 1998. No. 112. – Enabling power:Social Security Contributions and Benefits (Northern Ireland) Act 1992, ss. 122 (1) (a) (d), 129 (2) (4), 131 (1), 132 (4) (b), 133 92) (i), 171 (1) (3) (4) & S.I. 1995/2705 (NI.15), arts. 6 (5), 143 (2) (4) (b), 36 (2). – Issued:25.03.1998. Made:18.03.1998. Coming into operation:06.04.1998. Effect:S.R. 1987/459, 461; 1996/198; 1998/59 amended & S.R. 1997/354 revoked. – 12p. – 0 337 93089 9 £2.40

TERMS AND CONDITIONS OF EMPLOYMENT
Employment Rights (Increase of Limits) Order (Northern Ireland) 1998. No. 130. – Enabling power:S.I. 1996/1919 (NI. 16), arts, 23 (2), 63 (7), 154 (2), 158 (2), 159 (7), 231 (2), 251 (2) (3). – Issued:22.04.1998. Made:31.03.1998. Coming into force:01.04.1998. Effect:S.R. 1995/342 revoked. – 6p. – 0 337 93117 8 £1.55

Price/availability liable to change without notice

WEIGHTS AND MEASURES
Measuring Equipment (Liquid Fuel and Lubricants) Regulations (Northern Ireland) 1998. No. 113. – Enabling power:S.I. 1981/231 (N.I. 10), arts. 9 (1) (3), 10 (6), 13 (1). Issued:27.03.1998. Made: 27.03.1998. Coming into force: 20.04.1998. Effect:S.R. 1989/169 revoked. – 20p. – 0 337 93088 0 *£3.70*

Price/availability liable to change without notice

NUMERICAL LIST OF STATUTORY RULES OF NORTHERN IRELAND WITH SUBJECT HEADINGS

68	Magistrates' courts
	Road traffic and vehicles
88	Criminal procedure
89	Legal aid and advice
90	Legal aid and advice
94	Health and personal social services
95	Health and personal social services
104	Race relations
106	Sex discrimination
112	Housing
	Rates
	Social security
113	Weights and measures
114	Housing
115	Education
116	Road traffic and vehicles
117	Education
118	Education
119	
(C. 5)	Education
121	Health and personal social services
122	Health and personal social services
123	Health and personal social services
124	Agriculture
125	Health and safety
127	Employment and training
	Social security
128	Dangerous drugs
130	Terms and conditions of employment
133	Local government
136	Pensions
137	Pensions
138	Health and personal social services
139	Registered homes
140	Registered homes
141	Road and railway transport
142	Road and railway transport
143	Road and railway transport
144	Road and railway transport
146	Plant health
147	Planning
148	Harbours, docks, etc.
155	Lands tribunal

LIST OF COMMENCEMENT ORDERS

(C.)	(S.I).
5	119

ALPHABETICAL INDEX TO STATUTORY RULES

The index is cumulative, arranged by subject terms. The page references at the foot of the page refer to the pagination of the issues of the monthly lists.

Index

A

Advertisements: Control of: Planning	244
Agriculture: Beef carcase: Classification	97
Agriculture: Deseasonalisation premiums: Payments: Protection	45
Agriculture: Feeding stuffs	243
Agriculture: Hill livestock: Compensatory allowances	173
Animals: Bovine spongiform encephalopathy	45
Animals: Cattle: Identification: Enforcement	97
Animals: Products of animal origin: Import & export	173
Animals: Specified risk material	45
Animals: Zoonoses	45
Armed forces: Race relations: Industrial tribunals: Complaints	245
Armed forces: Sex dsicrimination: Industrial tribunals: Complaints	245

B

Balnamore: Level crossing	245
Beef bones	45
Beef carcase: Classification	97
Beef: Deseasonalisation premiums: Payments: Protection	45
Bones: Beef	45
Bovine spongiform encephalopathy	45
Bread & flour: Food	97

C

Canada: Social security: Contributions & industrial injuries	173
Carrickfergus: Harbours	97
Cattle: Identification: Enforcement	97
Charges: Drugs & appliances	243
Child support: Family law	45
Children's evidence: Criminal procedure	97
Coldagh: Level crossing	245
Companies: Accounts: Disclosure of directors' emoluments	45
Conservation: Scallops	173
Construction: Explosives	46
County courts: Rules	97
Courses: Drink-drive offenders: Designation of district	244, 245
Courts: County courts: Rules	97
Courts: Magistrates' courts: Domestic proceedings	46
Courts: Magistrates' courts: Drink-drive offenders: Courses	244
Courts: Magistrates' courts: Rules	46
Courts: Supreme Court, Northern Ireland: Procedure	47
Crime: Proceeds: Criminal Justice Act 1988: Countries & territories designated	243
Criminal justice: Serious fraud	97
Criminal procedure: Children's evidence	97
Criminal procedure: Proceeds of crime: Criminal Justice Act 1988: Countries & territories designated	243
Criminal procedure: Serious fraud	97
Curriculum: Irish: Key stages 3 & 4: Programmes of study & attainment targets: Irish speaking schools	243

Pages 45-47 Jan, 97-98 Feb., 173-174 Mar, 243-246 April

D

Damhead North: Level crossing 245
Dangerous drugs: Misuse of drugs 243
Deseasonalisation premiums: Payments: Protection: Agriculture 45
Drink-drive offenders: Courses: Designation of district 244, 245
Drugs & appliances: Charges 243
Drugs: Dangerous: Misuse of drugs 243

E

Education reform: 1989 Order: Commencement 243
Education: Curriculum: Irish: Key stages 3 & 4: Programmes of study & attainment targets: Irish speaking schools 243
Education: Individual pupil's achievements: Information 45
Education: Institutions of further education: Superannuation & compensation: Local government 98
Education: Pupil records 45
Education: Reform 243
Education: School admissions: Appeal tribunals 243
Education: Students: Awards 173
Education: Students: Loans 97, 173
Employment & training: New deal 243, 245
Employment rights: Increase of limits 245
European Communities: Cattle: Identification: Enforcement 97
European Communities: Products of animal origin: Import & export 173
Evidence: Children's: Criminal procedure 97
Explosives: Construction 46

F

Family law: Child support 45
Feeding stuffs 243
Flour & bread: Food 97
Food protection: Emergency prohibitions 98
Food safety: Specified risk material 45
Food: Beef bones 45
Food: Bread & flour 97
Foods: Welfare 174
Fraud: Serious: Criminal justice 97

G

General medical services 46
General medical services: Medical practitioners: Vocational training 46
Guaranteed minimum pensions: Increase 173

H

Harbours, docks, etc.: Ports: Disposals of land: Levy 243
Harbours: Carrickfergus 97
Harbours: Northern Ireland Fishery Harbour Authority: Accounts 173
Health & personal social services: Drugs & appliances: Charges 243
Health & personal social services: General medical services 46
Health & personal social services: North Down & Ards Community Health & Social Services Trust. Dissolution 243
Health & personal social services: Pharmaceutical services 46, 243
Health & personal social services: Resources: Assessment 243
Health & personal social services: Ulster Community & Hospitals Health & Social Services Trust 243
Health & personal social services: Ulster, North Down & Ards Hospitals Health & Social Services Trust: Disso-

Pages 45-47 Jan, 97-98 Feb., 173-174 Mar, 243-246 April

lution 244
Health & safety: Construction: Explosives 46
Health & safety: Fees 244
Health & safety: Offshore Noise & Electricity Regulations 173
Health & safety: Petroleum Act 1987: Modification 46
Health: Plants 98, 244
Hill livestock: Compensatory allowances 173
Housing benefit 244
Housing: Social security 46, 47
Housing: Social security: Lone parents 244, 245
Housing: Social security: New deal 46, 47

I

Incapacity for work: Social security 173
Industrial pollution: Control: Applications, appeals & registers 97
Industrial pollution: Control: Authorisation of processes 97
Industrial pollution: Control: Prescribed processes 97
Industrial tribunals: Complaints: Race relations: Armed forces 245
Industrial tribunals: Complaints: Sex discrimination: Armed forces 245
Irish: Curriculum: Key stages 3 & 4: Programmes of study & attainment targets: Irish speaking schools . . 243

J

Jobseeker's allowance 46

L

Landlord & tenant: Rents: Registered: Increase 97
Lands tribunal: Salaries 244
Legal advice & assistance 244
Legal aid & advice: Legal advice & assistance 244
Legal aid & advice: Legal aid: Assessment of resources 244
Legal aid: Assessment of resources 244
Level crossings: Balnamore 245
Level crossings: Coldagh 245
Level crossings: Damhead North 245
Level crossings: Macfinn 245
Local government: Superannuation 244
Local government: Superannuation & compensation: Institutions of further education 98
Lone parents: Social security 244, 245

M

Macfinn: Level crossing 245
Magistrates' courts: Domestic proceedings 46
Magistrates' courts: Drink-drive offenders: Courses 244, 245
Magistrates' courts: Rules 46
Measuring equipment: Capacity measures 174
Measuring equipment: Liquid fuel & lubricants 246
Medical practitioners: Vocational training 46
Misuse of drugs: Dangerous drugs 243
Motor vehicles: Construction & use 245

N

New deal: Miscellaneous provisions 243, 245
North Down & Ards Community Health & Social Services Trust: Dissolution 243

Pages 45-47 Jan, 97-98 Feb., 173-174 Mar, 243-246 April

Northern Ireland Fishery Harbour Authority: Accounts 173
Nursing homes 245

O

Offshore Noise & Electricity Regulations 173

P

Pensions: Guaranteed minimum: Increase 173
Pensions: Personal & occupational pension schemes: Miscellaneous amendments 46
Pensions: Social security: Money purchase contracted-out schemes: Class 1 contributions: Reduced rates . 244
Pensions: Social security: Personal pension schemes: Minimum contributions 244
Personal & occupational pension schemes: Miscellaneous amendments 46
Petroleum Act 1987: Modification: Health & safety 46
Pharmaceutical services 46, 243
Planning: Advertisements: Control of 244
Plants: Health 98, 244
Pollution: Industrial: Control: Applications, appeals & registers 97
Pollution: Industrial: Control: Authorisation of processes 97
Pollution: Industrial: Control: Prescribed processes 97
Ports: Disposals of land: Levy 243
Proceeds of crime: Criminal Justice Act 1988: Countries & territories designated 243
Products of animal origin: Import & export 173
Public health 98

R

Race relations: Industrial tribunals: Complaints: Armed forces 245
Race relations: Prescribed public bodies 98
Rates: Social security 46, 47
Rates: Social security: Lone parents 244, 245
Rates: Social security: New deal 46, 47
Registered homes: Nursing homes 245
Registered homes: Residential care homes 245
Registered rents: Increase 97
Rents: Registered: Increase 97
Residential care homes 245
Road & railway transport: Level crossing: Balnamore 245
Road & railway transport: Level crossing: Coldagh 245
Road & railway transport: Level crossing: Damhead North 245
Road & railway transport: Level crossing: Macfinn 245
Road traffic & vehicles: Drink-drive offenders: Courses 244, 245
Road traffic & vehicles: Motor vehicles: Construction & use 245
Roads: Street works: Supervisors & operatives: Qualifications 98

S

Salaries: Lands tribunal 244
Scallops: Conservation 173
School admissions: Appeal tribunals 243
Sea fisheries: Conservation: Scallops 173
Serious fraud: Criminal justice 97
Sex discrimination: Industrial tribunals: Complaints: Armed forces 245
Social fund winter fuel payment 47
Social security 46, 47
Social security: Claims & payments 47
Social security: Contributions & industrial injuries: Canada 173
Social security: Incapacity for work 173

Pages 45-47 Jan, 97-98 Feb., 173-174 Mar, 243-246 April

Social security: Jobseeker's allowance 46
Social security: Lone parents 244, 245
Social security: Money purchase contracted-out schemes: Class 1 contributions: Reduced rates 244
Social security: New deal 46, 47, 243, 245
Social security: Personal pension schemes: Minimum contributions 244
Social security: Social fund winter fuel payment 47
Specified risk material: Animals 45
Street works: Supervisors & operatives: Qualifications 98
Students: Awards 173
Students: Loans 97, 173
Superannuation & compensation: Institutions of further education: Local government 98
Superannuation: Local government 244
Supreme Court, Northern Ireland: Procedure 47

T

Terms & conditions of employment: Employment rights: Increase of limits 245

U

Ulster Community & Hospitals Health & Social Services Trust: Establishment 243
Ulster, North Down & Ards Hospitals Health & Social Services Trust: Dissolution 244

V

Veal: Deseasonalisation premiums: Payments: Protection 45
Vehicles: Motor: Construction & use 245

W

Weights & measures: Measuring equipment: Capacity measures 174
Weights & measures: Measuring equipment: Liquid fuel & lubricants 246
Welfare foods 174
Winter fuel payment: Social fund 47

Z

Zoonoses 45

Pages 45-47 Jan, 97-98 Feb., 173-174 Mar, 243-246 April

Stationery Office information and services

Stationery Office catalogues
The Stationery Office provides a complete bibliographic service for titles published by the Stationery Office or sold on an agency basis. The services ranges from a daily listing of new publications to annual catalogues and a database on CD-ROM. Full details are available from Bibliographic Services, The Stationery Office Ltd, PO Box 276, London SW8 5DT (tel 0171 873 8275, fax 0171 873 8463).

Publications Centre
This is the main warehouse and distribution centre for Stationery Office publications, and is the address for mail orders: The Stationery Office Ltd, PO Box 276, London SW8 5DT.

Bookshops
There are seven Stationery Office bookshops, in London, Edinburgh, Belfast, Bristol, Manchester, Birmingham and Cardiff (addresses on back cover). In other locations the Stationery Office is represented by our network of agents (see Yellow Pages: Booksellers).

World Wide Web
The Stationery Office National Publishing's Internet site contains information about publications and services, including the *Virtual Bookstore*, our on-line catalogue including an archive of Daily Lists and an ordering facility. The web site is at **http://www.national-publishing.co.uk**

Selected subscription service
For a single advance subscription (representing a considerable saving on the total price of publications), customers can be supplied automatically with one copy of most publications published by the Stationery Office (there are exceptions: details from address below). It is possible to break this down further into one or two of the following categories: Parliamentary, Non-Parliamentary, Statutory instruments. Further information and costs can be obtained from Selected Subscription Service, The Stationery Office Ltd, PO Box 276, London SW8 5DT (tel 0171 873 8409, fax 0171 873 8244).

Standing order service
This service is open to all Stationery Office account holders, and allows customers to receive automatically all publications they require in a specified subject area. There are some 4000 categories to choose from. Further information is available from Standing Orders Department, The Stationery Office Ltd, PO Box 29, St Crispins, Duke Street, Norwich NR3 1GN (tel 0870 600 5522, fax 0870 600 5533).

Subscriptions
Annual subscriptions may be placed for all periodicals. Further information may be obtained from Subscriptions, The Stationery Office Ltd, PO Box 276, London SW8 5DT (tel 0171 873 8499, fax 0171 873 8222) for Stationery Office publications, and from Agency Subscriptions for items sold but not published by the Stationery Office (tel 0171 873 8409, fax 0171 873 8244).

Trade terms
Booksellers who would like further information on the Stationery Office Ltd's trade terms and representatives should contact Sales Office, The Stationery Office Ltd, PO Box 276, London SW8 5DT (tel 0171 873 8404, fax 0171 873 8203).

Enquiries

The details given below are of services available in London and Norwich; customers may also contact the Stationery Office's bookshops and agents.

By post

To enquire about an order already placed, to enquire about accounts or to make a general enquiry .... The Stationery Office Ltd. PO Box 276 London SW8 5DT

By telephone

To make a general publications enquiry (Stationery Office titles) 0171 873 0011

Enquiries on agency publications
(sold but not published by the Stationery Office) 0171 873 8372
Enquiries from government departments 0171 873 8373/8367
To enquire about opening an account 01603 695711

Subscriptions (Parliamentary and non-Parliamentary) 0171 873 8499
Subscriptions (Agency publications) 0171 873 8409
Standing orders 0870 600 5522

Stationery Office bibliographic catalogues 0171 873 8275
London Gazette Office 0171 394 4580

By other means

Fax enquiries 0171 873 8247

Fax subscriptions 0171 873 8222

Fax standing orders 0870 600 5533

World Wide Web: http:/www.national-publishing.co.uk/

e-mail:book.enquiries@theso.co.uk

Orders

Stationery Office books can be ordered from

- **The Stationery Office Ltd. Publications Centre**
  PO Box 276
  London SW8 5DT (mail and telephone orders only)

  Telephone orders 0171 873 9090

  General enquiries 0171 873 0011

  Fax orders 0171 873 8200

  Fax standing orders 0870 600 5533

  Fax subscriptions (Stationery Office titles) 0171 873 8222

  Fax subscriptions (Agency titles) 0171 873 8244

- **Stationery Office bookshops** at

  123 Kingsway, **London** WC2B 6PQ 0171 242 6393 Fax 0171 242 6394

  68/69 Bull Street, **Birmingham** B4 6AD 0121 236 9696 Fax 0121 236 9699

  33 Wine Street, **Bristol** BS1 2BQ 0117 926 4306 Fax 0117 929 4515

  9-21 Princess Street, Albert Square, **Manchester** M60 8AS 0161 834 7201 Fax 0161 833 0634

  16 Arthur Street, **Belfast** BT1 4GD 01232 238451 Fax 01232 235401

  71 Lothian Road, **Edinburgh** EH3 9AZ 0131 228 4181 Fax 0131 622 7017

  The Stationery Office Oriel Bookshop, The Friary, **Cardiff** CF1 4AA 01222 395548 Fax 01222 384347

- Stationery Office bookshop agents (see Yellow pages: Booksellers)

- Through any good bookshop

The publications referred to in this catalogue shall be supplied to the customer only on the Stationery Office terms and conditions of sale (see p. xi-xii) and not on any additional terms which may be included with the customer's order.

Prices and availability are subject to alteration without notice

SI-CD - Statutory instruments on CD-ROM

Contains the full text and graphics of Statutory Instruments from 1987 onwards and a short form of Statutory Instruments from 1980 onwards. Updated six times a year.

An annual subscription costs £900.00 (excluding VAT in EC)

For further information please contact The Stationery Office Ltd. Electronic Publishing Sales:

Telephone No.   +44 (0) 171-873 8732
Fax No.   +44 (0) 171-873 8203

If you would like to place an order contact The Stationery Office Ltd. Subscriptions:

Telephone No.   +44 (0) 171-873 8499
Fax No.   +44 (0) 171-873 8222

British Standards

Now available from all Stationery Office Bookshops

The seven Stationery Bookshops are now official distributors for the British Standards Institution (BSI). The bookshops stock a range of British, European and international (ISO) standards, and can order and obtain any standard within 24 hours. The Stationery Office Bookshops are at:

123 Kingsway, **London** WC2B 6PQ
Tel 0171 242 6393 Fax 0171 242 6394

68/69 Bull Street, **Birmingham** B1 2HE
Tel 0121 236 9696 Fax 0121 236 9699

71 Lothian Road, **Edinburgh** EH3 9AZ
Tel 0131 479 3141 Fax 0131 479 3142

The Stationery Office Oriel Bookshop
The Friary, **Cardiff** CF1 4AA
Tel 01222 395548 Fax 01222 384347

16 Arthur Street, **Belfast** BT1 4GD
Tel 01232 238451 Fax 01232 235401

33 Wine Street, **Bristol** BS1 2BQ
Tel 0117 926 4306 Fax 0117 929 4515

9-21 Princess Street, **Manchester** M60 8AS
Tel 0161 834 7201 Fax 0161 833 0634
BSI Hotline 0161 834 4188

Our staff have been trained by BSI and can provide an informed service to help you determine which standards best suit your needs. British Standards promote quality in every sector of industry so make sure standards are playing their full part in your success.

Contact your nearest Stationery Office Bookshop for more details and to place your order.

THE STATIONERY OFFICE TERMS AND CONDITIONS OF SALE

DEFINITIONS

1.1 In the following and any other conditions included in the Contract, the expressions listed below shall have the meaning shown:

Expression	Meaning
The Seller (We, Us)	The Stationery Office Ltd. its staff, and authorised representatives and assignees.
The Customer (You)	whoever sends us the Order for the Goods.
Goods	the item fitting the description in your Order and as available from The Stationery Office's lists of items.
Price	that quoted in The Stationery Office's current price list plus any applicable VAT.
Force Majeure	any circumstances beyond our reasonable control, such as accidents, flood, fire or other natural disasters, and unlawful industrial disputes.
Contract	the agreement between us and you made by our acceptance of your Order.
Order	your request for the Goods.

APPLICABLE CONDITIONS

2.1 These are the only conditions which shall apply to the Contract. Any variations to them must be agreed in writing by our Head of Sales or Credit Controller.

ACCURACY OF DESCRIPTION

3.1 We shall only be liable to supply the Goods which you describe accurately in your Order.

3.2 When your Order does not accurately describe the Goods we will use our best endeavours to supply the correct Goods but you shall not rely on our skill and judgement in selecting these.

DELIVERY

4.1 You shall accept the Goods securely packaged at your address in the United Kingdom or Republic of Ireland, during normal business hours. Delivery in the United Kingdom shall be the later date of either 14 days from receiving your Order, or the publication date of the Goods.

4.2 Unless otherwise agreed we shall charge you a handling fee for delivery by mail or carrier.

4.3 We may charge you for the cost of delivery by any other method or to other countries.

4.4 Where we cannot deliver by the promised date we will promptly advise you of the reason. We may make a partial delivery of your Order where not all items are available. You have the right to return that partial delivery at our expense by the most economical method, within 5 working days of receiving it.

INABILITY TO SUPPLY

5.1 If we notify you in writing that we are unable to deliver the Goods as specified for Force Majeure or "out of stock" reasons, you shall allow us to deliver within a further reasonable time. What is a further reasonable time shall depend on the nature and duration of the force majeure or out of stock position.

5.2 You may return any Goods that are not delivered within that further reasonable time, but not within 14 days of being notified of inability to supply. On safe return of the goods in saleable condition we will cancel the invoice.

OWNERSHIP OF THE GOODS

6.1 The Goods remain our property until you pay for them, but you shall be responsible for their condition once they are delivered to your premises. You shall insure them to cover any risk this involves.

6.2 If you become insolvent we may take the Goods back at your expense and if necessary, may enter your premises to do so, or to inspect the Goods.

DAMAGE OR LOSS IN TRANSIT

7.1 We will replace at no extra cost any Goods damaged before or on delivery, if you notify us by telephone or in writing within 5 days of their receipt.

7.2 We will replace at no extra cost any Goods which have been lost in transit if you notify us by telephone or in writing within 21 days of us receiving your Order or the publication date of the Goods, whichever shall be the later.

REJECTION

8.1 We aim to take care to provide goods of a merchantable quality which are fit for their purpose and value for money. These Terms and Conditions show how we aim to do this, and do not affect your legal rights.

8.2 If you notify us by telephone within 5 working days of receipt of any Goods which are defective, and confirm this in writing at our request, and then return them at our expense stating the reason you are rejecting them, we will promptly replace them with Goods in an acceptable condition.

8.3 We will refund the price of any Goods which we are unable to replace with Goods in acceptable condition.

8.4 If you accurately described the Goods in your Order form you may within 5 days of receipt return any Goods that do not conform with your description. We will replace at no extra charge the Goods with Goods that correspond to your description.

PAYMENT

9.1 You shall pay our invoice for the Price of the Goods and any delivery charges, as defined in 4.2 and 4.3 above within 28 days of the date of our invoice, unless our Head of Sales or Credit Controller has agreed otherwise in writing.

9.2 Your payment shall be in sterling, free from any bank or transmission charge.

INTELLECTUAL PROPERTY RIGHTS

10.1 You shall protect our copyright and all other intellectual property rights in the Goods, while they remain your property.

10.2 You shall notify any subsequent owner of such rights in the Goods.

CANCELLATION

11.1 We shall stop despatching Goods against a Standing Order within 3 working days of receiving your written request to do so. You shall pay us for any Goods despatched in that period.

11.2 You shall not cancel Orders that we have already entered into our Order processing system.

ENFORCEMENT

12.1 Our failure to enforce any of these Conditions shall not prevent us from enforcing them at a later date.

12.2 If any Condition is found to be invalid, it shall not prevent all other Conditions being enforced.

HEADINGS

13.1 The headings to each of these Conditions is for guidance only and shall not affect their interpretation.

COMMUNICATIONS

14.1 Any notification, request or other communication required under these Conditions shall be in writing, including facsimile transmission, unless specified otherwise and addressed to the Enquiries Manager.

GOVERNING LAW

15.1 Unless Goods are purchased from the Belfast or Edinburgh Bookshops, the Contract shall be in the English language, governed by English Law and subject to the exclusive jurisdiction of the English courts.

15.2 Where Goods are purchased from the Belfast Bookshop, the Contract shall be in the English language, governed by Northern Ireland Law and subject to the exclusive jurisdiction of the Northern Ireland courts.

15.3 Where Goods are purchased from the Edinburgh Bookshop, the Contract shall be in the English language, governed by Scottish Law and subject to the exclusive jurisdiction of the Scottish courts.